COMMUNITY SCIENCE AND SUSTAINABLE COMMUNITY DEVELOPMENT

DR. KHUSHBOO GUPTA

Contents

Contents

FOREWORD

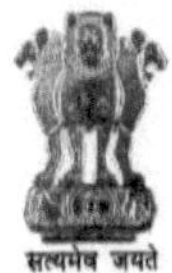

अध्यक्ष, लोक सभा
SPEAKER, LOK SABHA
INDIA

Message

Covid pandemic has caused widespread suffering to the humanity. The suffering is not just limited to loss of lives, but many have lost their livelihood too. In this context, new ways of thinking about sustainable development is needed. In view of this, the focus of government is on employment generation through skill development which is a sustainable way of increasing jobs and ensuring prosperity to the community. Governments are also working in this field to empower the communities and make them sustainable in different areas.

The book entitled "Community Science and Sustainable Community Development" edited by Dr. Khushboo Gupta makes a significant contribution in this context by covering different aspects relating to the subject matter and hence commendable.

I believe that the volume will provide useful knowledge to the youth and will certainly create awareness in the people about skill development, social innovation, self-employment and sustainable community development. I wish Dr. Gupta well for her future endeavours.

(Om Birla)

THE INSTITUTE OF CHARTERED ACCOUNTANTS OF INDIA
(Statutory Body Set up by an Act of Parliament)
Centre of Excellence, ICAI Bhawan, Village Chosla, Tehsil Chaksu, Distt. Jaipur
Website : www.icai.org ◈ Email : coejaipur@icai.in

Forward

It gives me immense pleasure to introduce this book entitled "Community Science and Sustainable Community Development" Which is very timely in the present context where not only our country India but the whole world is in epidemiological transition due to corona virus disease.

People are not only suffering from health issues but are going through economic crises as well. At this time utilization of teaching of community science for community development works as a strong foundation.

Community science is an area that focuses on scientific knowledge in the lifestyle of families and communities. Skill inculcation, social innovation, employment in different avenues can be given to people in different areas of community development that will create sustainability in community resulting a sustainable and self empower nation itself.

I appreciate the efforts taken by the expert group to bring out this book to promote and popularize the community science as a medium to provide self employment, economic sustainability and overall upliftment of the community.

I wish that this book encourage students in the field of community science to take up new research and set new examples. I wish Dr. Khushboo Gupta and her partners in this work a great success with this book and also look forward to similar efforts in future which would be useful to all stakeholders like academicians, policy makers and most importantly common people.

Prakash sharma

CA Prakash Sharma

Central Council Member of ICAI

H.O.: The Institute of Chartered Accountants of India, ICAI BHAWAN P.B.No.7100, Indraprastha Marg, New Delhi-110002
Telephones: 39893989, Gram: CICA, New Delhi
E.mail: icaiho@icai.org

PREFACE

Community Science is a discipline that is further classified into five sub disciplines namely (i) food and nutrition, (ii) clothing and textiles, (iii) human development, (iv) family resources management, (v) extension education and communication. Previously this discipline is known as Home Science and at that time people believes that if anyone wants to be a perfect home maker, she should take the Home Science as prime subject. But over the years this mind set of people changed and now the aspirants of Home Science are becoming nutritionist, dietitian, child psychologist, early childhood education trainers, fashion designers, ergonomist, etc. and are touching the sky in their respected fields.

In present era, the field of Community Science is experiencing much more awareness, new information and new developments. Old information needs to be revised and some new information needs to be added, therefore, this book has been designed and structured to update the current development in subject areas.

The book deals with the fundamentals of the society and how by using different approaches, a community or society can be developed in a sustainable manner, not only in terms of economic development but also in the areas of health, wellness, active ageing and nutrition. Chapters of this book particularly based on the topics related to skill inculcation, social innovation, community development through different sub disciples of community science, women participation in community development, use of new technology in community science and employment issues during covid-19 pandemic.

This book will be very useful for Indian and International students, academicians, public health specialists, community science specialists, community development professionals, programmers of national and international agencies, entrepreneurs and aspirants of new start ups/ enterprises. This book should be of interest to policy makers, bureaucrats, economists and community scientists and can be a reference material development industry.

This is my second book in the series of community upliftment. Previous book title is "Vridhopayogi Vyanjan: Vridhjano ke liye upcharatmak pak vidhiyan (year 2016)" that consists of more than 65 healthy food recipes prepared by myself alone, tailored with the nutritional needs of the geriatric population.

With great pleasure, I would like to extend my sincere thanks to all the learned contributors for the magnificent work they did in making sure that their timely response, excellent devoted contributions to detail and accuracy of information presented in this text along with their constant support and cooperation has made my task as editor a pleasure.

It is hoped that this book will stimulate discussions and generate helpful comments to improve future projects.

Happy reading and feedback awaited.

Dr. Khushboo Gupta
Assistant Professor
Trilok Singh TT College, Lakshmangarh,
Sikar, Rajasthan, India

ACKNOWLEDGEMENTS

It is indeed a great pleasure for me to express my profound gratitude to these eminent yet approachable personalities who helped me to bring this humble endeavour to its fruitful completion.

I am grateful to almighty God, who provided me an opportunity and ability to accomplish the great task, who in every moment of my life, always blessed me beyond my imagination, helped me in every difficult time and gave me strength and perseverance. Whatever I am today is just because of them.

I extend my thanks to Honorable Sh. Om ji Birla, Speaker, Lok Sabha, India and CA Prakash Sharma, Central Council member of The Institute of Chartered Accountants of India for their best wishes.

I deeply recognize the efforts by all authors for their contribution without whom this book will not look like what it is today. They deserve a special round of applause.

Finally, I acknowledge the sincere efforts of my family which has been the nucleus around which all my efforts have crystallized. No one can conquer without a strong base. I bow my head with great respect to my grandparents and hope that this work makes you proud. Thanks for your blessings. Words would fail to express my heartfelt veneration and deep sense of admiration to my loving siblings Er. Surbhee Gupta and Er. Saurabh Gupta for their love, affection, moral support, encouragement and help in every possible way to complete my work. Their unwavering faith in me has always been a source of constant inspiration for me.

I express deep and heartfelt obligation to my parents Mrs. Archana Gupta and Dr. Lok Mani Gupta for their patience, cordial affection, will power, blessings, moral support and for being my driving force. Their love provided inspiration and motivation, without which this work would not have been completed. They are the real architects of my life. They inspired me to build castles when all I had was a fistful of sand. They always stood by me during all thick and thin. Without their support, patience, sacrifice, forebearance and unalloyed love, this work would never have seen the light of the day.

I want to express feelings of utmost gratitude towards my parents-in-laws for their blessings. I owe thanks to a very special person my husband CA Dinesh Agrawal for being there for me at the end of the day. My husband's good spirits, patience, constant support and encouragement made it possible to accomplish this task which was initiated during the pandemic lockdown of second wave of corona virus disease. I appreciate my baby, my little girl Hemakshee for abiding my ignorance and the patience she showed during this endeavour. Her cute smile inspired me to go forward and her playful and naughty activities relaxed me during my tough times. Words would never say how grateful I am to both of you.

In the end, I want to express my sincere and deepest gratitude to everyone who, in their own way, directly or indirectly, have helped me to complete this book but could not have found separate names, so just in case: thank you to whom it may concern.

Dr. Khushboo Gupta
Sikar (Rajasthan)

Dr. Khushboo Gupta is a PhD Home Science (Food Science and Nutrition) from Banasthali Vidyapith, Newai, India. She has been teaching subject including food chemistry, food analysis, therapeutic nutrition, human nutrition, human physiology and community nutrition, etc. Presently she is working as Assistant Professor in Trilok Singh TT College, Laxmangarh, Sikar, Rajasthan.

She is MSc Gold medalist and had cleared UGC-NET and RPSC-SET examination. Dr Gupta holds Advance Diploma in French Language from Banasthali Vidyapith; Diploma in Naturopathy and Yoga (NDDY) from Gandhi Smarak Prakritik Chikitsa Samiti (Regd.), New Delhi; Certificate in Homeopathic Medicinal System conducted by Vardhman Mahaveer Open University, Kota and Certificate in Statistical Techniques and Applications. She has featured in several programs of All India Radio and Radio Banasthali (FM 90.4).

Dr. Khushboo actively involved in community activities especially those concerned with self-employment, health and wellness, optimum nutrition and how to improve quality of life of a person and family. She is the keynote speaker and founder of her YouTube channel "Dietitian Ki Salah" through which she provides education related to optimum health, wellness and nutrition to masses.

Dr. Gupta has published about more than 30 research papers in reputed national and international journals; 3 book chapters in three different edited books; 1 book and several news paper and magazine articles related to health, nutrition and new food product formulation. She presented her research work in more than 25 national and international conferences. Her research is primarily in the area of food processing entrepreneurial skill Inculcation and geriatric nutrition and her research on food formulation using RSM has culminated into the successful filing of a patent that has been published.

In past she had worked as Assistant Professor (Food and Nutrition) in Modi University, Laxmangarh, Sikar; worked as Master Trainer in Agriculture University, Kota. During her PhD she had worked as UGC- SRF in Banasthali Vidyapith, Newai. One feather in her cap is that she had worked as regular trainee dietitian in dietetics department of Post Graduate Institute of Medical Education and Research (PGIMER), Chandigarh and got her short-term attachment certificate. She won many awards in different seminars and conferences for her contribution in scientific world. Apart from them, she is rewarded with Teacher Honour award by Lions Club Kota South (September, 2017) and 'Award of Honour' given by All Rajasthan Qualified Homoeopathic Doctors Association in Homoeopathic Scientific Seminar, 2017

She is the life member of many reputed institutes i.e. Nutrition Society of India, Indian Dietetic Association, The Indian Science Congress Association and Institute of Scholars and giving her services for upliftment of community.

List of Contributors

1. **Adothu Lalitha**, M.Sc. Home Science (Extension and communication management), YFA-KVK, Madanapuram, Wanaparthy district, PJTSAU, Hyderabad, Telangana, India
2. **Ankita Kumari**, Scholar, Department of Development Communication and Extension, Lady Irwin College, New Delhi, India
3. **Anukriti**, Research Scholar, Department of Human Development and Family Studies, Babasaheb Bhimrao Ambedkar University A Central University, Lucknow, Uttar Predesh, India
4. **Avni Singhal**, Student - M. Design, School of Fashion Design & Technology, Amity University, Mumbai, Maharashtra, India
5. **Dinesh Agrawal**, Chartered Accountant, BP Kyal & Co. Sikar, Rajasthan, India
6. **Dr. Bilquis**, Associate Professor and Head (HDFS), College of Home Science, ANGRAU, Guntur, India
7. **Dr. Deepa Swamy**, Associate Professor, Govt Arts Girls College, Kota, Rajasthan, India
8. **Dr. Jinamoni Saikia**, Professor, Dept. of Human Development and Family Studies, College of Community Science, Assam Agricultural University, Jorhat-13, Assam, India
9. **Dr. Khushboo Gupta**, Assistant Professor, Trilok Singh TT College (Trilok Singh Shikshan & Anusandhan Sansthan), Lakshmangarh, Sikar, Rajasthan, India
10. **Dr. Khwairakpam Sharmila**, Assistant Professor, Department of Human Development and Family Studies, Babasaheb Bhimrao Ambedkar University, Lucknow, Uttar Pradesh, India
11. **Dr. L. Uma Devi**, Professor and Dean of Community Science, ANGRAU, Guntur, India
12. **Dr. Lok Mani Gupta**, Senior Homoeopathic Physician, Gupta Homoeo Clinic, Agrasen Bazar, Kota, Rajasthan, India
13. **Dr. Neetu Singh**, Associate Professor, Department of Human Development and Family Studies, School of Home Science Babasaheb Bhimrao Ambedkar (A Central) University, Lucknow, Uttar Pradesh, India
14. **Dr. Sarita Anand**, Associate Professor, Department of Development

Communication and Extension, Lady Irwin College, New Delhi, India

15. **Dr. Satish Kumar**, Assistant Professor, Faculty of Social Work, The Maharaja Sayajirao University of Baroda, Vadodara, Gujarat, India

16. **Dr. Shalini Agarwal**, Associate Professor, Department of Human Development and Family Studies, Babasaheb Bhimrao Ambedkar University, Lucknow, Uttar Pradesh, India

17. **Gayatri Prajapati**, Research Scholar, Department of Human Development and Family Studies, School of Home Science, Babasaheb Bhimrao Ambedkar University, Lucknow, India

18. **Gottemukkula Bhavani**, SMS (Agril. Extension), YFA-KVK, Madanapuram, Wanaparthy district, PJTSAU, Hyderabad, Telangana, India

19. **Harish Kumar Dhingra**, Assistant Professor, Mody University of Science and Technology, Rajasthan, Sikar, Lakshmangarh, Rajasthan, India

20. **Khwairakpam Sharmila**, Assistant Professor, Department of Human Development and Family Studies, School of Home Science, Babasaheb Bhimrao Ambedkar University, Lucknow, Uttar Pradesh, India

21. **Manisha Dhami**, Research Scholar, Human Development & Family Studies, Punjab Agricultural University, Ludhiana, Punjab, India

22. **Neetu Singh**, Associate Professor, Department of Human Development and Family Studies, Babasaheb Bhimrao Ambedkar University A Central University, Lucknow, Uttar Pradesh, India

23. **Neha Jain**, Research Scholar (Food Science and Nutrition), Banasthali Vidyapith, Newai, Rajasthan, India

24. **Neha Joshi**, Research Scholar, Human Development & Family Studies, Punjab Agricultural University, Ludhiana, Punjab, India

25. **Nidhi**, Research scholar, Department of Human Development and Family Studies, School of Home Science Babasaheb Bhimrao Ambedkar (A Central) University, Lucknow, Uttar Pradesh, India

26. **Poonam Verma**, Research Scholar, Department of Human Development and Family Studies, Babasaheb Bhimrao Ambedkar University, Lucknow, Uttar Pradesh, India

27. **Poppy Gogoi**, Ph.D., Dept. Of Human Development and Family Studies, College of Community Science, Assam Agricultural University, Jorhat-13, Assam, India

28. **Prarthana Kapadia**, Student - B. Design, School of Fashion Design & Technology, Amity University, Mumbai, Maharashtra, India

29. **Prof. (Dr.) M.N Parmar**, Professor, Faculty of Social Work, The Maharaja

Sayajirao University of Baroda, Vadodara, Gujarat, India

30. **Reema Ningthoujam**, Research Scholar, Mody University of Science and Technology, Rajasthan, Sikar, Lakshmangarh, Rajasthan, India

31. **Rondla Anitha,** SMS (Home Science), YFA-KVK, Madanapuram, Wanaparthy district, PJTSAU, Hyderabad, Telangana, India

32. **Saurabh Gupta**, Probationary Officer, UCO Bank, Shoping Centre, Kota, Rajasthan, India

33. **Seema Sharma**, Principal Extension Scientist, Human Development & Family Studies, Punjab Agricultural University, Ludhiana, Punjab, India

34. **Shalini Mohanty**, Assistant Professor, School of Fashion Design & Technology, Amity University, Mumbai, Maharashtra, India

35. **Syed Shakir Ali,** Senior Scientist and Head (Entomology), YFA-KVK, Madanapuram, Wanaparthy district, PJTSAU, Hyderabad, Telangana, India

If readers have any query related to any chapter of the book, kindly contact with the corresponding author of the chapter. Authors of the chapters are solely responsible for their work.

I

Sustainable Development to Sustainable Communities

Dr. Satish Kumar[1] and Prof. (Dr.) M.N Parmar[2]
[1]Assistant Professor, [2]Professor
Faculty of Social Work, The Maharaja Sayajirao University of Baroda,
Vadodara, Gujarat
Email Id: bodla_satish@yahoo.co.in; mnp.msu@gmail.com

Abstract

For the last three decades, International communities and policymakers crossed the world were very much concerned about the adverse effect of developmental efforts and human actions. As a response to the concern during the 1980s, the new concept of sustainable development was emerged to fulfil the materials needs of the present generation without compromising the need of future generations along with maintaining the integrity and sustainability of the environment. The World Commission on Environment and Development (1987) defines sustainable development as "Development that meets the needs of the present without compromising the ability of future generations to meet their own needs". As per the report, the scale of change may be so high that there might be a coordination and cooperation problems. Globally, the difficulties associated with political and culture association provide the key reason to advocate the concept of sustainable communities.

Yanarella and Levine (1992a:769) stated that if we would like to achieve sustainability on a wide scale, all efforts should be directed to develop the sustainable communities that may be the most effective way of revealing the possibility that sustainability, precisely because it places the concept of sustainability. By applying the efforts towards sustainable community development, the sustainability will be more visible because the efforts at the local and micro-level can be more focused and changes can be observed and perceived immediately as compared to macro-level efforts or interventions. At the local level where the outcomes of environmental declination can be easily and directly perceived, the developmental efforts/ intervention plan can be initiated by ensuring the participation of social organizations where the people are well aware of their needs, resources, strengths, opportunities, and challenges. In the context of a sustainable community, a social worker as a part of a team can play a significant role to mobilize the community resources and active people participation because of its field-based component which is totally based on fieldwork practice, intervention, and exposure.

In the context of the present paper, it can be concluded that communities are different in terms of environmental issues availability of resources, educational & income status , social & infrastructure development and climatic conditions which can be well addressed and utilized by applying the various community need-based intervention approaches. As the concept of sustainable community development focused on flexibility and need-based intervention, a community-level approach will allow to formulate a policies that provides more developmental opportunities to particular places or locality.

Key Words: Sustainable Development, Sustainable Community, Resources.

Introduction

In the current century, how to manage and mobilization the various resources productively & adequatelyis the main challenge. The worldwide efforts towards economic growth and development result from the imbalances in environmental and social aspects along with other areas. When there is an imbalance in any area or field, it generally leads towards a crisis and when a difficulty of any kind occurs, a community need to work together to respond appropriately and timely to the problem in order to find out the most suitable solution to the crisis/problem. On one hand, the decision-making efforts/capacity of the community may fulfil the well-being needs of the community and also may create future opportunities from the crisis.

Sustainability is an ideal goal of a society or community which largely depends on the economic condition, environmental conditions, and social factors of a society or each community. The term "Sustainable Community" is widely used nowadays. The term is not just used or is related to the economic development but also focus on quality of life, protection of environmental and natural resources along with other aspects of human life. A community that has balanced socio-economic & environmental conditions, resources are mobilized and properly managed can be sustainable.The sustainable community can be a mobile society that evolve itself with occurred challenges, time to time adopt new alternatives plan to convert available resources into community assets.

Constraints of development

To create or develop the balancing spheres between socio-economic and environmental aspects is the main goal of the sustainable community. Economic growth which is not just the sole aim of sustainable communities but it includes the each aspects of human life which promote quality of life along with equity and fair deal.

The model of sustainable communityadvocates that to preserve the present resources for the use of future generations is a crucial need for sustainable communities and in the development process the main role need to play bythe present generation. The outcomes of various researches show that primarily Inclusiveness, Connectivity, Equity, Security & Inclusiveness are the main five constraints to sustainable development.

The details of sustainable constraints are as follows.

Firstly, as per the inclusiveness constraints, the development is inclusive in nature because it always ensures the social well-being of the people along with environmental, health, and economic activities. In the course of the development process when inclusiveness is practiced there should be no threat or danger to the existing eco system. Secondly, under sustainable development, it is very much essential to understand the connectivity between human and natural systems. Once, we are able to understand the connectivity we will be able to know more holistically the impactof development .The lack of understanding of connectivity will be a major constrain in the development path of community development. Thirdly, equity is also an important factor in sustainable community development that can be ensured through fair distribution of resources which will enable the community to sustain its resources for the future generation. Fourthly, under sustainable development for regeneration and restoration of resources maintaining life-supporting ecosystems is also essential. There is a need to consume the currently available resources within limitations so that the sustainability and availability of theresources can be ensured in future also.

Finally, keeping in view the human-centred nature of sustainable development security is another constraint that society needs to develop within. In the development process, there is also a need to ensure that life-supporting systems should be preserved in such a way that the livelihood and survival of human beings is not threatened. The last constraints postulate that the development needs to be pursued within these premises.

Challenges faced by communities

The major challenges faced by the communities are as follows.

1. **Limitation of Resources.** In rural areas, resource limitation especially human resources is an unavoidable problem. The brain drain has become phenomena recently in many communities especially rural areas where young people or the talent decide to leave their communities/countries to live or work in another place that providing them a better quality of life. Due to a lack of the right kind of talent at the community level, a community is not able to reach its fullest potential development.

2. **Climate Change & Natural Resource Management:** In the current time, the climate change is a matter of concern for everyone because it has a direct effect on eco system, health condition and lives of millions of people. In many communities, it is observed the natural resources are not managed properly by the community due to a lack of expertise and

knowledge in the field.

3. **Lack of People Participation:** It is observed that there is a lack of people participation and involvement, especially the young generation in the community development activities. To ensure community participation, there is a need to generate interest in self-reliant communities.

4. **Lack of Good Governance:** Lack of good governance is observed as another challenge in the path ofsocio-economic development of a community. Good governance can be a main force in formulating a holistic action plan and implementation can be ensured through a smart approach and political will to achieve the "Sustainable Community" goal. Government also need to be sensitive about the people concern while framing and development plan and also need to ensure people participation in decision making.

5. **Inefficiency of Technology:** Now a day's technology can play an important role in community development whereas the inefficiency of the use of technology can be a hurdle. The use of technology may facilitate the community development process bur need to be conscious about the too much use of it because it may disturb the natural shape of current traditional good practices.

6. **Time-Taking Process:** For sustainable community development incremental changes are essentials which can be ensured through theco-operation and co-ordination of various stakeholders which may include the local self-government, civil societies, community and faith based organizations, NGOs etc. during the whole process a proper planning, organization, consultation , braining storming, capacity building is required which is again a very lengthy and time consuming process.

7. **Social Norms and Belief:** To great extent community behavior and social practices are influenced/conditioned by social norms and beliefs which may be currently relevant or not depending on current prevailing social norms and beliefs. Many a time we need to modify or challenge the prevailing norms and practices in order to ensure the relevant changespertaining to the sustainability of the community. The evaluation process of norms may enable the community to preserve its culture and identity.

Sustainable communities

Sustainability means 'to maintain; keep in existence, keep going; prolong'. The developmental goals of any communitycan be translated through the application part of sustainability. The societal system is complicated in nature and there are variety of elements which are intervened and interconnected (via various sub systems) in such a way that facilitate the community into in pursues of its developmental goals. Therefore, concept of sustainability should be able to meet the needs of the present generation without compromising the ability of future generations to meet their own needs.

Sustainable communities are considered mobile societies which generally evolve themselves, opt new developmental approaches or modify old one and seek to convert its resources into assets. Under sustainable development efforts are made to increase the control over developmental decisionby the community members by applying 'bottom up' approach which leads to active people participation and effective decision making. (Gibbs, 1994:106-107).

Sustainable communities may work as a medium through which the community resources, economic production, and commerce activities can be decentralized and localized. The outcome of the whole process will come in the form of the social surplus of the local economy which will lead towards the self-sufficiency and self-enhancement communities.

The sustainability of a community basically can be ensured by providing the multiple resources in the form of safe drinking water, health and safety, resource mobilization so on and by the proper waste management system. In a sustainable community, resource consumption is balanced by resources assimilated by the ecosystem, and a community generally not able to reach its goal of sustainability when the consumption of resources is more as compare to its renewal and the community produces more wastes.

The imbalances in socio-economic &ecological areas occurs when economic development exerts pressure on these spheres which may gradually leads to a crises in the form of climate change, cultural erosion which ultimately negatively affect the entire humanity/society. The occurred crisis demands thesociety/community to respond and manage appropriately by making appropriate decisions/interventions and by re-evaluating the community priorities. In the crisis management process, there is always a need to ensure active people participation, evolving mind-sets, cooperation, and coordination.

To develop the ability among the community members to make development choice is the ultimate goal of sustainable community development which must respect the relationship between the three "E's" which are as follows.

1. **Economy** – The economic activity should be planned in such a way that it serves the common economic goal, should be self-renewing in nature, and outcome should lead to build local assets and self-reliance community.
2. **Ecology** – Ecology is an essential part of human lives, nature has its own limits, and it is the responsibility of communities to protect and building natural assets so that the resources will remain in a balanced manner.
3. **Equity** – To ensure sustainable communities it is very much essential that equal opportunities for participation in activities and decision making should be provided. It is also important to ensure the equal distribution of resources & benefits to all without any kind of discrimination.

The term "sustainable community" grew out of the related discourses of "sustainability" and "sustainable development". The concept has incorporated at politicians and policymakers in the developmental agenda at local, national, and internationallevel. Sustainable communities planned, built, or modified their developmental activities and initiatives in such a way that promotes sustainable living with special emphasises on economic growth, social equity, ecological balances, urban infrastructure development, and good governance.

The main stress of various definitions of sustainable community development is on the importance of balancing the environmental concerns and development objectives. The panning of developmental activities and initiatives should be in the direction of enhancing the local social relationships. But many community-related studies documented the serious gaps in local-oriented actions and efforts of social organization (Wilkinson, 1991), especially in rural areas. There are evidences that all communities do act and take immediate remedial steps in reaction to perceived issues and challenges.

From sustainable development to sustainable communities

The current developmental experiences show that country wise political, socio-economic and cultural difficulties are associated with the goal achievement of sustainability. At the international level the issues and challenges faced & associated with development agenda populates one of the key justifications for sustainable communities. The requirement of change is so great that the coordination and cooperation at various level is essential.

The unsustainable practices where much attention is not given to the ecological imbalances and fall below the threshold of public attention efforts should be made on strengthening the socio- economic, & environmental conditions directed towards sustainability communities.

The issues and challenges faced at various levels can be responded appropriately, by focusing on sustainability practices at the grass root level where changes can immediately observed and interventions are most noticeable. To create a "sustainable society" the extremely difficult task is to develop the political will which is one of the important component in the implementation of sustainable practices.

Moreover, as Yanarella and Levine (1992a:769) observe & stated that sustainability can be achieved on a broader scale and the possibility can be demonstrated only through sustainable community development efforts. In nutshell, it can be stated that the roots of sustainable development are based on communities where the advantage of flexibility always prevails. The Communities are different in terms of socio-economic conditions, environmental issues, natural and human resources, levels of education, income, livelihood opportunities, social development, and physical infrastructure, and climatic conditions. It would be an injustice to advocate for one universal approach or model of sustainable development rather, it should be based on local requirements, sensitive to the local opportunities, community felt needs and places or locality specific.

Sustainable community and resource asset model

Resources are always considered crucial to the development of any community and may be an important asset for the community. Generally, there are many community resources like human, financial, cultural, natural, infrastructure along with others may exist in tangible or intangible which may directly or indirectly play an important role in converting the sustainable communities. According to the 'Resource Asset Model' sustainable community development can be ensured by developing the abilities to control on their lives, resources and developing capacities how convert the current resources need into assets.

At the community level, the development goals can be achieved by applying the appropriate mobilization strategies. The interplay between networks and collaboration along with interweaving of the economic, social, and environmental sphere can be used as a tool to convert the resources into assets. The available resources can be useful only when the community members know how to manage, mobilize and channel resources effectively. Resources can be mobilized to achieve a sustainable community through education and sensitization, financial & technical support, appropriate government policies or legislation, constructive use of mass media, and people participation.

Interactional approach to sustainable community development

According to the interactional perspective, the community are the composition of various more or less distinct inter-related social units through which each element assume or express particular interests and are interrelated in one or another way. Since all the components are interrelated and have similar socio-economic interests, they will be able to develop similar perspectives and similar definitions of the same situation. As Maines (1989:110) puts it, "Those who participate in common channels of communication tend to develop common outlooks."

If the various stakeholders/components hold different interests and perspectives or having very little or no experience in dealing with the interest of each other, they will be able to work jointly and mutually satisfactory solutions to the problem will not be there.

Further, if such a situation is repeated over time, the interaction pattern will be suppressed in nature. To tackle such kinds of issues, there will be a need to establish communicative ties among the various interactional unitswhich can be ensured by developing a well-accepted mechanism. Efforts should be made by the community organizer or mobilizer that individual unit interest should not supersede the interest of the whole group or not to pursue any single interest, but the general community interest instead. However, the community units are fragile and varies over time. Another inevitably characterized of the community is power struggles and conflict, which may be the potential barrier to sustainability.

The whole sustainable community development model will probably require the politics of possibility. The politics may require collaboration among civil societies, CBOs VOs, community forums, and a willingness to engage in meaningful must be there.

Conclusions

In conclusion, it can be stated that the root of sustainable development is in place-based communities where flexibility is the main advantage. All communities are very in nature and composition about the socio-economic condition, environmental issues, natural and human resources, levels of income, social and infrastructure development, and climatic change. A community-based approach will allow the government/community mobilizer to design the policies that are sensitive to the community development opportunities.

Sustainable communities can be ensured or promoted by applying a five-step approach which may include assessment of current conditions, trend analyses, Create vision statements, formulation and implementation of the action plan.

References

1. Achelle Hollander & Nathan Kahl. (2010)Engineering, Social Justice, and Sustainable Community Development, the National Academics Press.
2. Chamberland & Denys. (1994). The Social Challenges of Sustainable Community Planning. **Plan Canada**, July: 137-43.
3. Chris Maser. (1996).Development: Principles and Concepts, CRC Press.
4. Claude Henry, Johan Rockström & Nicholas Stern. (2020). Standing Up for a Sustainable World: Voices of Change, Edward Elgar Publisher.
5. Jim Lotz, & Gertrude Anne.(2003). Sustainable People: A New Approach to Community Development, Cape Breton University Press.
6. Sandra Velthuis. (2015). Sustainable Communities: A Funding Handbook for Community-Led Groups, The Wheel, with the support of the Environmental Protection Agency publisher

7. Pushpanjali Malla. (2021).Sustainable Community Development: People's Participation is a must, Himalayan Publication House.

8. Sim Van der Ryn, & Peter Calthorpe. (2008), Sustainable Communities: A New Design Synthesis for Cities, Suburbs and Towns, New Catalyst Books.

II

Opportunities and Challenges in Skill Development

Rondla Anitha[1], Gottemukkula Bhavani[2], Adothu Lalitha[3] and Syed Shakir Ali[4]

[1]SMS (Home Science), [2]SMS (Agril.Extension), [3]M.sc Home Science (Extension and communication management) and [4]Senior Scientist and Head (Entomology)

YFA-KVK, Madanapuram, Wanaparthy District, PJTSAU, Hyderabad, India

Email: rondla.anitha@gmail.com

Abstract

Skill development is considered as one of the critical input for creation of jobs and their reducing unemployment in India. Development of skill helps in improving the career of youth and build confidence in them in taking up of any challenges. India has demographic advantage with more than 50 percent of younger population compares to any other developed country. But at the same time India is facing a huge challenge in employing their youth as a result leaving most of them unemployment. In this scenario Skill development is the best initiative taken by the Government of India that identify and trained the young age group for improvement their employability. In this paper we tried to chalk out the challenges faced in skill development and at the same time identified opportunities in skill development through different government institutes. There are two skill developmental schemes that focus to addresses the prevailing challenges for youth in India and provide opportunity for employbility through different public and private partnership.

Key words: Skill development, Government initiatives, Opportunities and challenges.

Introduction

Skill development is the most important tool that empower individual and aids in overall development of the Nation. Its safeguard the future of the unempoloyed youth in developing countries in India. There is every need for the government and for the policy makers to educate the individual to the aspect of skill development. If the government can reach large no of audience, that can enhance the employability in todays globalization. Education and skill if they go hand on hand that can improve the competencies of the individuals to reach the essential requirements of the industries in which they can serve. In India there exist four levels of skills as per the National Skill Development Corporation (NSDC). These four levels of skills are supported with the degree and length of coaching is required.

Skill Level I: its called Semiskilled which meant that the skills cannot be acquired enough through Vocational Courses, it requires specific intervention on the job. *Skill Level II:* It is called, this kind of skill level are very specific to particular job undertaken and same as the skill level I this skill level also may not be acquired enough through any special skill development courses. *Skill Level III:* It is Highly Skilled, the name itself suggest that this kind of skill level is associated with high industrial operations and require special technical aspects and again not acquired enough through any professional degree. *Skill Level IV:* It is Highly proficient kind of skill level where in this kind of skill level implies competencies derived through training , research and analysis with specialization in particular area and again no inheritable through degree.

India is well known for its youngest populated nation of the world. With these advantage it could benefit over other populated country in the world till 2040 (Planning Commission, 2013).With this younger population India has an increased scope to enhance the production and productivity of labour requirement compared to any other developing and developed countries in the world (Chenoy, 2012).

With this added advantage in our country we still face the challenge in the area of skill development and acquirement. According to world bank enterprise survey which was condcuted in 2014 in india reflects that only 36 percent of the firms are offering training for the full time job requirement but every year around double the percentage (64 %) newcomers come out.

India got lot of educational infrastructure which provides sophisticated learning experiences to the students, but the student with greater education with less or no skills cannot reach their desired careers. As it is mentioned earlier that education and skill development should go hand on hand to enhance the full potential of individual in his career. With the increased use of technology in the country that brings immense change in the skill development because of the fast change in technology, students mainly who graduated from their degrees required to proper skill training for their desired career development hence skill is required at every age in every degree irrespective of either educated or illiterate.

Challenges of Skill Development

Acquisition of Skill is essential challenge for accelerated growth and providing employment opportunities to the younger generation. Some of major key challenges are mentioned below.

1. *Problem in setting up of institutions:*

In India the major challenge is setting up of educational and training institution mainly in cities. According to censes 2011 the number of people living in the remote areas are higher than the people living in the cities. Mainly concentrating on youngest population in which not every individual has an opportunity to migrate from villages to cities for education and training to acquire job specific skills. This geographical set up of institutes are in cities lacks to address more number of individual bridge a gap in skill development mainly in developing countries like India.

2. Lack of Infrastructure:

The most important challenge is availability of Proper basic infrastructure facilities for skill development programs. Infrastructures facilities are play crucial role in appropriate execution of the skill and in capacity building programs. But most of the skill development institutions are lacking infrastructure facilities like there is no proper equipments, upgraded machines and tools etc where in workers find themselves deficient in skills when they employed because they were trained under outdated machine are not available in addition to this lack of industry linkages is also a major challenge in addressing the courier development.

3. Lack of Mobilization:

Another tremendous challenging task of skill development is the registration of Youth for Skill Developmental courses. Attitude of younger generation related to skill development are need to be improved as per the present day requirement because they lack the managerial skills. Hence there is a poor recognition obtaining poor salaries in the field situation. There are many students who are economically poor not able to pay fee for skill development courses. Therefore those students may not aware about the government ongoing scheme for skill development which also leads to a low mobility towards such programs. Even though some students got opportunities in industries but they were not satisfied with their salaries which also leads to low mobilization. Like in advanced countries India also need to focus on the skill development and presentation strategies so that youth get mobilize towards such programs and get benefitted.

4. Lack of Private Sector Participation:

Private sector in India has a huge scope in providing employability but its participation in providing required skills is limited. As the population in rural India is more, participation of private sector in addressing such population for their professional development need to be taken care, which stood as one of the major challenges in skill development sector.

5. Direct admission without Assessment:

Most of the training institutes are directly taking admission without pre assessment or entrance exam. Unevenly choosen skill development courses which lead to skills mismatch between the interest and abilities of the students as a results students are unable to perform effectively in their selected profession and also dropout occurs. Therefore industries and other placement institutes should match the institution requirement.

6. Lack of consistency in skill

There exist a huge gap between the Skill possessed by the youth and actual skills required for industrial profile, which is prevailing challenge that results in unemployment among youth in India. This brings to our consideration that including the industrial professionals in planning and designing of the training curriculum is most significant step need to be taken to remove the in consistency of skills require.

Opportunities

Demographic advantage is one of the interesting aspect compared to the developing countries like U.K, U.S.A. and Japan by recognizing such a greater opportunity, Indian government started to set up skill India movement which has the potential to bridge the skill gap in specific and increase the national economy in general. As per the National Higher Education Commission assessed that during the next 20 years, the labour force in the industrial world is expected to decline by 4 percent in other developed countries compared to India which will increase by 32 percent. The list below depicts the some of the skill India movement through different program interventions:

1. Pradhan Mantri Kaushal Vikas Yojana:

National Skill Development Corporation implemented Pradhan Mantri Kaushal Vikas Yojana (PMKVY) flagship scheme of the Ministry of Skill Development & Entrepreneurship (MSDE), which was launched on 16 July 2015. This Skill Certification Scheme where in this Yojana undertake huge number of youth to help them to get into industries thereby improving the rural economy. The scheme provides help to the youth in the form of skill training relevant to the skills that are required for the industries. National occupational standard and qualification packs are provide basis for the training program for various specific skills. The other advantage of the scheme is it certify the individual by assessing their prior skill and experience through Recognition of Prior Learning.

Key elements of PMKVY:

1. Vocational Training Courses- This Vocational Training courses will benefit school dropout or unemployed youth. The youth trained under this short term are assessed and shell be linked with industries associated with the skills learned by the assistance of Training Partners. The fee for the concerned training provided by the government for the individual who enrolled under this Vocational Training Courses.
2. Recognition of Prior Learning (RPL)- it is a component where in the individual with Prior knowledge on particular skill or any working experiences, can get assessed and certified under RPL.
3. Special Projects- under PMKVY there is another advantage called special project component where in it provide training in the premises of government, corporate and industries on special skills under special areas which are not defined under National Occupational Standards (NOSs).
4. Kaushal and Rojgar Mela- Melas or community gatherings aid in facilitating to acquire additional knowledge that which helps in better career development. PMKVY provide this mobilization process for every six month through press and media coverage which ask for active participation by the youth.

5. Placement- PMKVY Training Centers provide placement linkages for building career opportunities as per the demanded market. The training facilities to improve aptitude and specific knowledge skills and the placement opportunity at the right place that help in enhancing the employability in the country. In addition to this Training institutes will also support to Entrepreneurship Development.

6. Monitoring- PMKVY Training centers developed latest and efficient monitoring tools or methodologies such as self-inspection reporting, call

validations, Unanticipated visits. Continuous Monitoring is done through the Skills Development Management System (SDMS).

Table 1: Details of No. of candidates Enrolled, Trained, Assessed, Passed and Certified under PMKVY.

PMKVY	Enrolled	Trained	Assessed	Passed	Certified
Short term project	3417496	3361853	3172794	2836809	28359801
RPL	3322065	32225029	2913679	2737342	2734671
Special project	154120	145520	125814	107073	106805

(Source- website of PMKVY)

2. *Deen Dayal Upadhaya Grameen Kaushalaya Yojna:*

As mentioned previously in this chapter, according to 2011 censes of India, the nation got the advantage with highest younger population compared to any other developed countries. This 2011 censes reflects the point that the number of rural youth are more compared to the urban area, therefore with this advantage if the rural youth get trained in India that increase rural employment and economy thereafter.

Ministry of Rural Development launched Deen Dayal Upadhaya Grameen Kaushal Yojana (DDU-GKY) Antyodaya Diwas on 25th September 2014.This scheme focuses especially on Rural younger generation between the ages of 15 and 35 years from poor families.

Table 2: Detailes of candidates Trained, Placed, Assessed and Certified under DDU-GKY.

Financial year	Trained	Placed	Assessed	Certified	Centres	Traders
2014-2015	43038	21446	NA	NA	-	-
2015-2016	236471	1,09,512	NA	NA	-	-
2016-2017	349155	185045	244631	171251	654	329
2017-2018	142597	63787	121849	99546	726	381
2018-2019	241178	137494	180826	146328	1196	433
2019-2020	238693	150119	128981	99921	1220	433
2020-2021 till Nov 2020	3839	32414	924	648	1703	502

(Source-website of DDU-GKY)

Benefits of DDU-GKY

There are no fee charges for training under taken for registration for examination for certificate and placements with an idea to benefit as many as youth possible.

Conclusion

Skill development is the foremost important aspects need to be considering in present fast change in technological environment. So to make the effective changes in this direction there is a need for involvement and coordination among all the stakeholders to make skill India movement successful. The government should reach as many as individual possible through the skill development programs. The main aim of the Skill development initiatives is it not only provides skill training to get placement at industrial level but also support entrepreneurship development among the enroll individuals. The National skill development corporation should also focus on the challenges that hinder skill development through organized Skill development schemes that place vital role in enhancing the booming ecosystem for first generation entrepreneurs in the country.

References

1. Abhishek Kumar, 2017. Skill India: Opportunities & Challenges.*International Journal of Engineering and Management Research.* 7(3):66-68.
2. Anita Swain and Sunita Swain.2020. Skill Development in India: Challenges and Opportunities.*International Journal of Scientific and Engineeering Development.*3(6):238-245.
3. Easha sherma and Sakshi sethi.2015.Skill Development:Opportunities & Challenges in India. Giyan Jyotie-journal.5(1).
4. GOI 2009. National Skill Developmen Policy, Goverment of india,http://www. Skill development. gov.in/resources/national-skill-dev-policy
5. Lavina Sharma and Asha nagendra, 2016. Skill Development in India: Challenges and Opportunities. *Indian Journal of Science and Technology,* 9(48).

6. Maclean,R. 2013. Skill development for inclusive and sustainable growth in developing Asia- Pacific,Dordrecht:Springer

7. Planning commission (2013). Twelth Five Year Plan(2012-2017) Employment and Skill Development,Planning Commission,Government of india,140.

8. Ravi Kumar,S. 2000. Skill Development in India - Present Scenario and Challenges.*International Journal of Humanities &Social science Studies.* 5(1):27-35

III

Skilling Food Industry to Utilize Moringa

Neha Jain

Research Scholar (Food Science and Nutrition), Banasthali Vidyapith

Email: 282nehajain@gmail.com

Abstract

*Moringa oleifera*is named as the "Miracle tree". The co-products of *Moringa oleifera* are like fresh flowers, pods, and fresh green leaves that are loaded with nutrients like antioxidants, vitamins, anti-inflammatory and minerals. They are sufficiently packed in the RDA(recommended dietary allowances). This tree is indigenous to India, flourishes in different type of soil and in tropical zones of India. This plant can stand drought conditions, but water tension affects its growth. This tree has several bioactive chemical compounds in it, and is helpful for humans and animal consumption also. It is used in treating a lot of diseases and also used as raw material in some industries. The food industries have motivating challenge forward: incorporating *Moringa* as an ingredient, as an alternate for classical preservatives, antioxidant and simultaneously preparing variety of food commodities, having high nutritional value, and should be ideal for certain communities where individuals are at high risk of malnutrition.The tree provides an environmentally-safe substitute for the sustainable development of the food, health and technology industries. Conclusively, the present study is an attempt to provide scientific knowledge on *Moringa oleifera* regarding the agronomic and botanical characterization, medicinal and agro-industrial uses, that allow supporting the varied properties attributed to it.

Keywords: industrial uses, medicinal uses, miracle tree, *Moringa oleifera*.

Introduction

Moringa oleifera is also popular by the name of "The Miracle Tree", "Horseradish-tree", "Drumstick tree", "Ben oil tree" and extensively distributed species of the family *Moringaceae*, having magnificient number of therapeutic uses as well as good nutritional value all over the globe (Mughalet al., 1999; Somali et al.,1984). The leaves, bark, seeds, roots, flowers and saps are extensively used in traditional medicine. Whereas, green leaves of the plant are utilized in the form of food for nutrition (Stohs and Hartman, 2015).It is important to exploit all the nutrients of this amazing tree for various purposes. Almost every part of *Moringa* holds some potential value and uses. The fresh pods as well as green leaves are exploited by the population in form of food stuff. Researches shows that *Moringa* contains vitamin C, vitamin A, calcium, potassium and proteins as compared to those in carrots, bananas, milk and eggs respectively (Fahey, 2005). Leaves are the most used part of *Moringa* plant because of its high vitamin, polyphenol, flavonoid, carotenoid, phenolic acid, isothiocyanate, phenolic acid, tannin and saponin content. The leaves, roots and bark, these parts of tree are used for treating and preventing over 300 ailments (National Institutes of Health-NIH, 2018). Several studies revealed, in vivo as well as in vitro, have validated the pharmacological properties of drumstick tree. These pharmacological properties can be described by the presence of high range of bioactive compounds (Leone et al, 2015). *M. oleifera* has been probably one of the underused tropical crops. *Moringa* is considered as a valued source of nutrients for the individuals of every age group (Price, 2000).

In undeveloped countries, people commonly lack many important nutrients in their diet. As *Moringa* leaves are rich in antioxidants and other nutrients, and this is why leaves are utilized for medicinal purposes and for human nutrition (Popoola and Obembe, 2013).

Botanical description

This is known as an eco-friendly tree because of its application in issues related to socio-environment (Anwar et al., 2007). India is the primary producer of *Moringa oleifera* having yearly production of about 2.2 to 2,4 million tonnes from an area of 43600 ha which leads around 50 tonnes of productivity per ha. Due to varied genotypes and the diversified geographical area, Tamil Nadu is considered as a pioneering state of India (Sekhar et al., 2017). The genus *Moringa* cover 13 species which are distributed throughout northeast Africa southwest Asia, Madagascar and southwest Africa. These species of *M. oleifera* has been grown across the globe, specifically in Florida, Asia, Latin America, Pacific Islands and Caribbean (Fahey, 2005).

The tree can be cultivated in both the regions subtropical and tropical with the temperature between 25-35^{0}C. Sandy and loamy soil are best suitable with slightly alkaline or slightly acidic pH. It requires a net rainfall of 250-3000mm (Thurber and Fahey, 2009).*Moringa* plants can even be grown where there is lack of rain and could be grown in soils with low or bad-quality, leading to small changes in the nutritional composition of all its part (Fahey 2005; Anwar et al., 2007).

Due to its high germination rates, the "direct-seeding method" is followed. Germination of seeds take place between 5-12 days after seeding. These can be buried in the soil at a depth of 2 cm. Containers can also be used to propagate *Moringa* (Aslam et al., 2005).

Moringa a potential tree for value addition

Several researches have revealed the favourable effects of drumstick tree on human beings (Stohs and Hartman, 2015). Owing to the versatile uses of *Moringa*, many herbal preparations gleaned from anecdotal evidence are manufactured to cure number of diseases. *Moringa* powder used in homes as nutritional supplement. With *Moringa* oil and leaves, soaps, tea bags, body lotions and creams are produced (De-heer, 2011). *Moringa* leaf powder poses a significant antioxidant, antidyslipidemic and antihyperglycemic effect when administered orally, without any adverse effect (Nambiar et al., 2010).

Moringa oil, *Moringa* leaf tablets, *Moringa* energy bites, *Moringa* energy drops, bio instant soup, oil cakes, *Moringa* honey, *Moringa* chips,

Moringa Idly powder, *Moringa* capsules. These are various value added food products of *Moringa* prepared using *Moringa* seeds, leaves, pods, seed kernel, flowers and gums as raw material (Sandeep et al., 2019).

Details of some food products developed by incorporating Moringa oleifera (Joshi and Verma., 2017) -

1. Mathri (salted crackers)– Deep frying method was used
2. Aloo Tikki (Potato pattice) – Shallow frying
3. Khaman – Steaming
4. Biscuit – Baking

Recipe for Cookies:

Ingredients: whole wheat flour (100gm), *Moringa* powder (40gm), Millet flour (60gm), Clarified butter (90gm), Honey (10ml), Palm sugar (30gm), Milk powder (2gm).

Method: Sun dry *Moringa* to convert this in powder form. Cream together all the mentioned ingredients. Make a dough and regrigerate for 15mins. Give them a round shape to make cookies. Bake at 170^{0}C for 12-15 mins. Cool at room temperature and store in an air tight container (Manviel, 2019).

Medicinal uses

Leaves of this tree are studied most widely. The incredible medicinal usage of the tree that are claimed by various cultures as well as communities based on their actual experiences, are gradually being proved by science now. (Kasolo et al., 2010). The tree can be helpful in treating more than 300 diseases as this tree is often referred as panacea. Indians and Africans use *Moringa* as herbal medicine for treating some diseases. *Moringa* have good phytochemicals in it, and this makes it a good medicinal agent (Gopalakrishnan et al., 2016).

Several research studies found that *M. oleifera* possess crucial nutrients that are amino acids, omega 3 fatty acids and omega 6 fatty acids, vitamins, beta-carotene, antioxidants, minerals and anti-inflammatory nutrients (Kasolo et al., 2010; Hsu et al., 2006). Drumstick tree have vital role in medicinal, nutritional and therapeutic properties (Al-Kharusi et al., 2009).

Studies have reported that these leaves are beneficial in various chronic diseases that includes non-alcoholic liver disease, hypertension, diabetes, hypercholesterolemia, insulin resistance, cancer and inflammation (Vergara et al., 2017). Drumstick tree is a nutritious plant, and it is ideal for treating malnutrition in developing countries (Debajyoti et al., 2017; Gopalakrishnan et al., 2016). *M. oleifera* holds considerable anti-cancer and anti-diabetic properties. (Gopalakrishnan et al., 2016).This tree is also considered as laxative, anti-hypertensive, hypoglycemic and many more functions effects as well (Dong et al., 2019).Leaves of this tree helps in treating malaria, typhoid with decreasing role of the individual's inflammatory response of the body (Waterman et al., 2014; Donkor et al., 2015; Udosen et al., 2016; Dondee et al., 2016).

Studies reported that this tree can help in the regulation of thyroid hormoneand improving renal as well hepatic functions (Tahiliani and Kar., 2000; Benett et al., 2003). Leaves also protect against oxidative stress (Anwar et al., 2007), inflammation (Mahajan et al., 2009), hepatic fibrosis (Hamza, 2010), liver damage (Pari and Kumar., 2002), hypercholesterolemia (Halaby et al., 2013; Okwari et al., 2013), bacterial activity (Peter et al., 2011), cancer (Anwar et al., 2007) and liver injury (Efiong et al., 2013).

Moringa oleifera as a sustainable resource

Drumstick tree is an alternative for products developed chemically, turning down the risk related with the buildup of chemical compounds that are non-biodegradable and are injurious for earthlings and environmental wellbeing. Because of these numerous applications, it is considered as ecologically viable (Sanchez-Martin et al., 2010; Okuda et al., 2001).Therefore, *Moringa oleifera*considered as a sustainable resource for food industry, biotech, medical sciences, animal-farming because it has been mainly cultivated as food source for both human and animal (Brilhante et al., 2017).

Moringa in food industries

Presence of various nutrients as well as secondary and some minor metabolites, *Moringa* can be used as raw material in food industry. *Moringa* have ability to take off harmful materials from water thus can be used in industries to remove impurities and unwanted materials from water

(Aney et al., 2009).

Due to its antimicrobial activity, leaves of this tree can be served as a substitute for antibiotics in various industries (Melesse et al., 2012).*Moringa* have high concentration of antioxidants, due to which oil extracted from *Moringa* and its mature leaves should be used as a preservative and as a food fortificant in industries (Bijina et al., 2011; Oyeyinka & Oyeyinka., 2016).*Moringa* have potential application in dairy industries due to the presence of aspartic, cysteine and protease-dependent calcium ions (Pontual et al., 2012).

Conclusion

The analysis on *M. oleifera* is neverthelessto achieve importance in India. *Moringa* being a miracle tree is locally available. This plant has to be cultivated in the areas where the optimum growth of the plant is favored by the climatic conditions. From this perspective, highest yield may be achieved from its various parts. This will be used for the welfare of the mankind. The demand of *Moringa* and its products, which should be value added, is rising day by day because of its high nutritional content and medicinal importance.

References

1. Al-Kharusi, L. M., Elmardi, M. O., Ali, A., Al-Said, F. A. J., Abdelbasit, K. M., & Al-Rawahi, S. (2009). Effect of mineral and organic fertilizers on the chemical characteristics and quality of date fruits. *International Journal of Agriculture and Biology*, 11, 290-296.
2. Aney, J. S., Rashmi, T., Maushumi, K., & Kiran, B. (2009). Pharmacological and pharmaceutical potential of Moringa oleifera: a review. *Journal of Pharmacy Research*, 2(9), 1424-1426.
3. Anwar, F., Latif, S., Ashraf, M., & Gilani, A. H. (2007). *Moringa oleifera*: a food plant with multiple medicinal uses. *Phytotherapy Research: An International Journal Devoted to Pharmacological and Toxicological Evaluation of Natural Product Derivatives*, 21(1), 17-25.
4. Anwar, F., Latif, S., Ashraf, M., & Gilani, A. H. (2007). *Moringa oleifera*: a food plant with multiple medicinal uses. *Phytotherapy Research: An International Journal Devoted to Pharmacological and Toxicological*

Evaluation of Natural Product Derivatives, 21(1), 17-25.

5. Aslam, M., Anwar, F., Nadeem, R., Rashid, U., Kazi, T. G., & Nadeem, M. (2005). Mineral composition of *Moringa oleifera* leaves and pods from different regions of Punjab, Pakistan. *Asian Journal of Plant Sciences*, 417-421.

6. Bennett, R. N., Mellon, F. A., Foidl, N., Pratt, J. H., Dupont, M. S., Perkins, L., & Kroon, P. A. (2003). Profiling glucosinolates and phenolics in vegetative and reproductive tissues of the multi-purpose trees *Moringa oleifera* L.(horseradish tree) and Moringa stenopetala L. *Journal of agricultural and food chemistry, 51*(12), 3546-3553.

7. Bijina, B., Chellappan, S., Krishna, J. G., Basheer, S. M., Elyas, K. K., Bahkali, A. H., & Chandrasekaran, M. (2011). Protease inhibitor from Moringa oleifera with potential for use as therapeutic drug and as seafood preservative. *Saudi journal of biological sciences, 18*(3), 273-281.

8. Brilhante, R. S. N., Sales, J. A., Pereira, V. S., Castelo, D. D. S. C. M., de Aguiar Cordeiro, R., de Souza Sampaio, C. M., ... & Rocha, M. F. G. (2017). Research advances on the multiple uses of *Moringa oleifera*: A sustainable alternative for socially neglected population. *Asian Pacific journal of tropical medicine, 10*(7), 621-630.

9. De-Heer, N. E. A. (2011). Formulation and sensory evaluation of herb tea from *Moringa oleifera*, Hibiscus sabdariffa and Cymbopogon citratus. M.Sc. Thesis (Ghana: Kwame Nkrumah University of Science and Technology).

10. Debajyoti, D., Dipsundar, S., Dinesh, B., Chandreyee, R., Sanatan, R., & Jayram, H. (2017). *Moringa olifera* (shigru): a miracle tree for its nutritional, ethnomedicinal and therapeutic importance. *International Journal of Development Research, 7*(11), 16823-16827.

11. Dondee, K., Bootprom, P., Saiphet, B., Borkaew, P., Klubsri, C., & Somsak, V. (2016). Antimalarial activities of *Moringa oleifera* leaf extract against Plasmodium berghei ANKA infection in ICR mice. *International Journal of Innovative Research In Medical Science, 1*(5), 194-201.

12. Dong, X., Guo, X., Hu, Y. (2019). Summary of studies on traditional Chinese medicine properties of overseas plant medicine *Moringa* leaves. Glob Tradit Chinese Med 12(1):149–153 (10. 3969/ j.issn.1674-1749.2019.01.050)

13. Donkor, A. M., Oduro-Mensah, D., Ani, E., Ankamah, E., Nsiah, S., Mensah, D. E., & Kusi, K. A. (2015). In vitro anti-plasmodial activity of aqueous and ethanolic extracts of *Moringa oleifera* and Phyllanthus amarus.

14. Efiong, E. E., Igile, G. O., Mgbeje, B. I. A., Otu, E. A., & Ebong, P. E. (2013). Hepatoprotective and anti-diabetic effect of combined extracts of *Moringa oleifera* and Vernonia amygdalina in streptozotocin-induced diabetic albino Wistar rats. *Journal of Diabetes and Endocrinology*, 4(4), 45-50.

15. Fahey, J. W. (2005). *Moringa oleifera*: a review of the medical evidence for its nutritional, therapeutic, and prophylactic properties. Part 1. *Trees for life Journal*, 1(5), 1-15.

16. Gopalakrishnan, L., Doriya, K., & Kumar, D. S. (2016). *Moringa oleifera*: A review on nutritive importance and its medicinal application. *Food science and human wellness*, 5(2), 49-56.

17. Halaby, M. S., Metwally, E. M., & Omar, A. A. (2013). Effect of *Moringa oleifera* on serum lipids and kidney function of hyperlipidemic rats. Journal of Apllied Sciences Research, 9, 5189-5198.

18. Hamza, A. A. (2010). Ameliorative effects of *Moringa oleifera Lam* seed extract on liver fibrosis in rats. *Food and Chemical Toxicology*, 48(1), 345-355.

19. Hsu, R., Midcap, S., Arbainsyah, D. W. L. (2006). *Moringa oleifera*: Medicinal and socio-economical uses. *International Course on Economic Botany, National Herbarium Leiden*, the Netherlands.

20. Joshi, P., & Varma, K. (2017). Preparation of Value Added Products from Dehydrated Drumstick Leaves. *Online Int. Interdiscip. J*, 7, 41-48.

21. Kasolo, J. N., Bimenya, G. S., Ojok, L., Ochieng, J., & Ogwal-Okeng, J. (2010). Phytochemicals and uses of *Moringa oleifera* leaves in Ugandan rural communities.*Journal of Medicinal Plants Research*,4, 753-7.

22. Leone, A., Spada, A., Battezzati, A., Schiraldi, A., Aristil, J., & Bertoli, S. (2015). Cultivation, genetic, ethnopharmacology, phytochemistry and pharmacology of *Moringa oleifera* leaves: An overview. *International journal of molecular sciences*, 16(6), 12791-12835.

23. Mahajan, S. G., Banerjee, A., Chauhan, B. F., Padh, H., Nivsarkar, M., & Mehta, A. A. (2009). Inhibitory effect of n-butanol fraction of *Moringa oleifera Lam.* seeds on ovalbumin-induced airway inflammation in a guinea pig model of asthma. *International journal of toxicology*, 28(6), 519-527.

24. Manivel, K. (2019). Nutritional and Sensory Evaluation of Moringa Oleifera Cookies. *Indian Journal of Public Health Research & Development*, 10(2).

25. Melesse, A., Steingass, H., Boguhn, J., Schollenberger, M., & Rodehutscord, M. (2012). Effects of elevation and season on nutrient composition of leaves and green pods of Moringa stenopetala and Moringa oleifera. *Agroforestry systems, 86*(3), 505-518.

26. Mughal, M. H., Ali, G., Srivastava, P. S., & Iqbal, M. (1999). Improvement of drumstick (*Moringa* pterygosperma Gaertn.)–a unique source of food and medicine through tissue culture. *Hamdard Med, 42*(1), 37-42.

27. Nambiar, V. S., Guin, P., Parnami, S., & Daniel, M. (2010). Impact of antioxidants from drumstick leaves on the lipid profile of hyperlipidemics. *Journal of Herbal Medicine and Toxicology, 4*(1), 165-172.

28. National Institutes of Health (NIH) (2008). NIH Record Vol LX, No. 6 (New York: NIH).www.nih.gov.

29. Okuda, T., Baes, A. U., Nishijima, W., & Okada, M. (2001). Isolation and characterization of coagulant extracted from *Moringa oleifera* seed by salt solution. *Water research, 35*(2), 405-410.

30. Okwari, O., Dasofunjo, K., Asuk, A., Alagwu, E., & Mokwe, C. (2013). Anti-hypercholesterolemic and hepatoprotective effect of aqueous leaf extract of *Moringa oleifera* in rats fed with thermoxidized palm oil diet. International Journal of Pharmacy and Biological Sciences, 8, 57-62.

31. Oyeyinka, A. T., & Oyeyinka, S. A. (2018). Moringa oleifera as a food fortificant: Recent trends and prospects. *Journal of the Saudi Society of Agricultural Sciences, 17*(2), 127-136.

32. Pari, L., & Kumar, N. A. (2002). Hepatoprotective activity of *Moringa oleifera* on antitubercular drug-induced liver damage in rats. *Journal of Medicinal Food, 5*(3), 171-177.

33. Peter, A., Walter, A., Wagai, S., & Joseph, O. (2011). Antibacterial activity of Moringa oleifera and *Moringa* stenopetala methanol and n-hexane seed extracts on bacteria implicated in water borne diseases.

34. Pontual, E. V., Carvalho, B. E., Bezerra, R. S., Coelho, L. C., Napoleão, T. H., & Paiva, P. M. (2012). Caseinolytic and milk-clotting activities from Moringa oleifera flowers. *Food Chemistry, 135*(3), 1848-1854.

35. Popoola, J. O., & Obembe, O. O. (2013). Local knowledge, use pattern and geographical distribution of *Moringa oleifera Lam.*(Moringaceae) in Nigeria. *Journal of Ethnopharmacology, 150*(2), 682-691.

36. Price,M. L. (2000). The *Moringa* Tree. Echo Technical note. Echo, Florida, USA, 12.

37. Rebecca, H. S. U., Sharon, M., Arbainsyah, A., & Lucienne, D. (2006). *Moringa oleifera*: medicinal and socio-economic uses. *International Course*

on Economic Botany. National Herbarium Leiden, Netherlands, 2-6.

38. Sánchez-Martín, J., Ghebremichael, K., & Beltrán-Heredia, J. (2010). Comparison of single-step and two-step purified coagulants from *Moringa oleifera* seed for turbidity and DOC removal. *Bioresource technology, 101*(15), 6259-6261.

39. Sandeep, G., Anitha, T., Vijayalatha, K. R., & Sadasakthi, A. (2019). *Moringa* for nutritional security (Moringa oleifera Lam.). *International Journal of Botany, 4,* 21-24.

40. Sekhar, C., Venkatesan, N., Vidhyavathi, A., & Murugananthi, M. (2017). Post harvest processing of Moringa and socio-economic appraisal of *Moringa* orchards in Tamil Nadu. *International Journal of Horticulture, 7.*

41. Somali, M. A., Bajneid, M. A., & Al-Fhaimani, S. S. (1984). Chemical composition and characteristics of *Moringa* peregrina seeds and seeds oil. *Journal of the American Oil Chemists' Society, 61*(1), 85-86.

42. Stohs, S. J., & Hartman, M. J. (2015). Review of the safety and efficacy of *Moringa oleifera. Phytotherapy Research, 29*(6), 796-804.

43. Tahiliani, P., & Kar, A. (2000). Role of *Moringa oleifera* leaf extract in the regulation of thyroid hormone status in adult male and female rats. *Pharmacological research, 41*(3), 319-323.

44. Thurber, M. D., & Fahey, J. W. (2009). Adoption of *Moringa oleifera* to combat under-nutrition viewed through the lens of the "Diffusion of Innovations" theory. *Ecology of food and nutrition, 48*(3), 212-225.

45. Udosen, I. E., Okwori, A. E. J., Ijebor, J. A., Jonson, P. O., & Adikwu, T. I. (2016). Effects of *Moringa oleifera* leaf tea on salmonella typhi and Escherichia Coli. *Journal or Dental and Medical Sciences, 15*(3), 62-66.

46. Vergara-Jimenez, M., Almatrafi, M. M., & Fernandez, M. L. (2017). Bioactive components in *Moringa oleifera* leaves protect against chronic disease. *Antioxidants, 6*(4), 91.

47. Waterman, C., Cheng, D. M., Rojas-Silva, P., Poulev, A., Dreifus, J., Lila, M. A., & Raskin, I. (2014). Stable, water extractable isothiocyanates from *Moringa oleifera* leaves attenuate inflammation in vitro. *Phytochemistry, 103,* 114-122.

IV

Empowerment of Youth via Skill Inculcation Trainings in Food Processing Sector

Khushboo Gupta[1], Saurabh Gupta[2], Dinesh Agrawal[3]
[1]Assistant Professor, [2]Probationary Officer, [3]Chartered Accountant
[1]Trilok Singh TT College (Trilok Singh Shikshan &Anusandhan Sansthan), Lakshmangarh, Sikar (Rajasthan), India; [2]UCO Bank, Shoping Centre, Kota (Rajasthan), India; [3]BP Kyal & Co. Sikar (Rajasthan), India
Email Id: drkhushboogupta2017@gmail.com

Abstract

Unemployment of youth is the biggest challenge for our country India. About 60% of Indian population is engaged in agriculture or agriculture based activities, thus it is the maineconomic action however because of various post-harvest misfortunes (i.e., loss of food quality, loss of food esteems, poor storage spaces, poor appropriation of food, and so on), farmers can't make legitimate profit from their produced crops. Indian food processing sector is fifth in terms of creation, utilization, exports and anticipated growth. Rural youth are educated but not properly skilled due to unavailability of training institutes near the production sites.Food processing sector is known as 'sunrise sector' which has direct link between agriculture and consumer. Various departments and Ministries of India provide trainings in food processing and preservation to inculcate the required skills, so that they can start a new enterprise.Legitimate training in food handling and valueaddition can make boom in employment, which eventually cause youth strengthening, confidence building, increased individual income and their way of living.

Key words: Food processing sector, Food processing and preservation, Entrepreneurial skills, Skill development

Introduction

India is the world's second biggest food producer next to China and has the capability of being the greatest on the planet. India is a farm-based country where more than 60% inhabitants rely on agriculture and agro based activities for their livelihood. Agricultural base of India is quite strong but the wastage of crops produced is very high and preparing of produced crop in food products is very low. Food processing and preservation contributes a major role in economy of India (Singh et al, 2012; Tiwari et al, 2016). Researches indicated that only 14% of total population is linkedto agro processing sector directly besides India being the largest producer of grain, cereals and pulses of numerous varieties (Bidar and Bhawani, 2015). Processing and preservation of produced agriculture crops not only reduce the wastage of crops but also creates the chances of entrepreneurship (income generation). The role of agro-based firms improves in relation to the development of rural and backward people (Perwez, 2017). Empowered employees increase execution mostly through identifying work processes in community-based businesses, which are considered to be a significant instrument for recognizing potential among marginal and underprivileged groups (Fernandez and Moldogazeiv 2013).

The majority of the world's adolescents live and work in rural areas, yet most developing countries' rural labour markets do not provide adequate nice work (FAO, 2013). In 2012, the global youth unemployment rate was 12.4%, about three times greater than the adult unemployment rate (ILO, 2013).

Sanjeeb Hazarika's expedition to learn about the motivational aspect of planning and its impact on starting a business in rural areas found that employment in the units had grown at a rate of 23 percent. 63 percent of entrepreneurs have improved their administrative talents through various trainings, and 59 percent have refurbished themselves with the assistance of truly exceptional mentors, 52% of respondents could productively designate accessible assets.

A multi-delayed way to deal with business advancement including a macro economic climate, abilities and work market arrangements that work with the school-to-work progress, rights at work, youth business venture and social assurance of youthful workers is essential. Molding powerful arrangements for decent work for youngsters at home and about movement – requires the commitment of government, employees' organizations and trade unions in friendly discourse. Advancing and incentivizing youth cooperation in the agrosector will give truly necessary work freedoms to rural youth, and helps strengthen food security at the family and national levels (FAO, 2013). For country development, it is important to acquire youth standard of advancement by grooming their abilities. Exceptionally little endeavors and essential preparing with respect to foundation and sustenance of enterprises can propel rustic individuals for making them as entrepreneurs. Rustic youth are not well equipped and skilledlike urban youth. In the present scenario, it is important among youth to inculcate vocational skills.

As a result, it has become necessary to concentrate on total skill development in order to become a great power and effectively address our demographic dividend, or human resource.

Three types of crops, i.e., Rabi, Kharif and Jayad are produced in India due to different climatic conditions. Farmers produced the crops and sell them as it is in Government mandies due to the lack of knowledge regarding processing, preservation and value addition of produced crops (Tiwari et al, 2017). Basic education regarding food processing and preservation along with the inculcation of skills not only reduce the wastage of produced food crops but also be helpful in enhancing the quality of life of the farmers. If farmers or rural people at grass root level have the processing and preservation skills they can start their own enterprise and may improve their socio-economic status. Thus the inculcation skills related to different aspects of foods as well as knowledge about technical and economical support will be very beneficial to youth. This conceptual review will be helpful to provide the knowledge which is required to start a new enterprise at small scale level.

Training

Training can be defined as the act of instilling or improving a person's knowledge and abilities in order for them to do a successful job (Meena et al, 2012). It is a type of interaction that consists of a series of encounters, or a progression of learning chances, in which trainees are exposed to specific materials, objects, or events in a very methodical manner. A strong and dynamic food processing sector contributes significantly to agricultural diversification, improved value addition opportunities, and surpluses for agro-food export (Merchant, 2008). Processed food industry is divided into two broad segments, (i) primary processed food items and (ii) value added processed food items.

"The key segments in the Food Processing sector are as follows-

1. _Fruits and vegetable_:

This segment includes fresh fruits, vegetables, dry fruits (eg- raisins, cashew), processed and packaged fruits and vegetables (such as- jams, jelly, pickle, sauce, food, paste, juice, concentrates, potato flour, canned fruit and vegetables).

2. _Dairy products_:

This segment includes pasteurized milk, milk powder, ice cream powder, condensed milk, infant foods, butter, ghee, cheese, cream, mawa, ice cream, kulfi and other dairy products.

3. _Meat and marine products_:

Meat products segment includes butchered, processed, preserved and canned poultry, mutton, pork, beef and others. Marine products segment includes sundried, artificially dehydrated, radiation preserved, processed, preserved and canned fish.

4. _Grains and oil seeds_:

This segment includes milling of flour, rice, pulses, wheat and other grains. It also includes processing and manufacturing of breakfastcereals, flour mixes and dough and other readymade powders (idli mix, dosa mix and gulab jamun).

5. *Packaged foods*:

This segment includes spices, snacks and savouries, ready-to-eat (RTE) and ready-to-cook (RTC) meals, beverages, chocolate and non-chocolate based confectionery, biscuits and bakery items.

6. *Beverages*:

This segment includes distilled alcoholic beverages, wines, beer, soft drinks, mineral water and other non-alcoholic beverages."

The demand of healthy value added and packaged food items are increasing day by day due to various reasons, hence, convincing skill enhancement trainings are required to tap the potential of these segments. There is a dire need to enhance innovation and improve quality of the value added food items and the training is essential to develop skilled work force who are capable of performing their work well. In India, central government, state government and numerous institutions are working in the sector of skill development.

Various Indian ministries and departments run following schemes, training and vocational education programmes related to agriculture, food processing & preservation, self help groups and entrepreneurshipdevelopment:-

1. Ministry of Agriculture and Farmers Welfare

(i) Department of Agriculture Research & Education provides training in horticultural augmentation, use of farming machinery and apparatus, soil-conservationtraining centers, LFQC&TI, NPPTI,cooperative education & training. The objective gatherings for this plan are the Persons occupied with agricultural institutions and backing administrations, individual from cooperatives and farmers.

(ii) Department of Animal Husbandry, Dairy& Fisheries provide training under the university stream, various under-graduate, postgraduate and Ph.D. courses are offered. The target groups for this scheme are the students with qualifications as under university stream of education.

2. <u>Ministry of Food Processing Industries</u>

(I) Grants are being given to NGOs to setting up of Food Processing and Training Centers (FPTCs). The objective gatherings for this plan are people living in provincial regions with inclination towards women, SC, ST and other vulnerable sections of society.

(ii) Institutions like Central Food Technology Research Institute, Paddy Processing Research Center, PHTC, and Council of Entrepreneurial Development Program (EDP) are likewise running instructional classes. The objective gatherings for this plan are essentially people working in food processing companies.

3. <u>Ministry of Micro, Small and Medium Enterprises</u>

(i) Entrepreneurship development programme for workers.

(ii) Small Industries Development Organization conducts skill development programme to educate unemployed youth.

(iii) Management development programme for entrepreneurs.

4. <u>Department of Women and Child Development</u>

(I) Support to Training and Employment Program for Women (STEP) plot gives refreshed abilities and new information to poor and assetless women in customary areas

(ii) Swalamban (beforehand NORAD) scheme normally trains helpless womenin non-conventional exchanges.

(iii) Training in home scale safeguarding of fruits and vegetables (by Community Food and Nutrition Extension Units (CFNEUs). Target group of this plan includes homemakers and juvenile young women to promote safeguarding, and utilization of soil-grown products that truly gives necessary micronutrients as well as essential abilities, which could be valuable for income generation purposes.

(iv) Central Social Welfare Board: Programs of this board are coordinated by voluntary associations to prepare women in attractive exchanges likewise to overhaul their abilities for getting profitable business opportunities.

(v) Women Empowerment Program in a joint effort with IGNOU (Training program on 'Empoweringwomen through SHG's). Objective of this program is to arrange women into powerful Self Help Groups.

"According to Apprentices Act (1961) different professional courses canvassed in the space of agribusiness arepoultry production, fisheries/ fish processing, dairying, sericulture, apiculture, gardening, plant insurance, agrarian synthetics, inland fisheries, crop plantation and management, seed production innovation, swine production, vegetable seed production, medicinal and sweet-smelling (aromatic) plant industry, sheep and goat husbandry, fix and upkeep of power driven farm hardware, veterinary pharmacist-cum-artificial insemination assistant, agro based food industry (crop, animal & feed based), post harvest innovation, fish seed production, fishing innovation, horticulture, soil preservation, crop development/ creation" (Goel, 2011).

In our country, Ministry of Food Processing Industries and Indian Council of Agricultural Research (ICAR) are the major bodies providing skill development training in the sector of food and agriculture. ICAR conduct different training programmes for farmers, women and youth through KrishiVigyan Kendra (KVK).

Skill development trainings in KVK

Food processing unit is a finished unit that can deal with end-to-end processing.Handling requires a group of laborers who know about all aspects of hygiene, sanitation standards and consistence norms and guidelines. They additionally need to cling to these principles to stay away from misfortunes during bundling and transportation. Frequently, there is an inclination to depend on intermediaries to back off the cycle. This can be avoided, if the farmers are in complete control of dealing with the store network.

Training is provided in the form of demonstration, exhibition, theoreticalknowledge of the subject, practical training and industrial visits.Topics that can be covered during the training programme are as follows:

(i) basics of food and nutrition, (ii) food processing techniques, their use and importance,(iii) advances in food processing technologies,(iv) different machinery required for food processing, (v) market analysis for food items, market value and market survey, marketing of food items and their production cost, (vi) communication and market skills required to start up a new enterprise, (vii) food regulation in India, rules and regulations of food safety standard authority of India (FSSAI), (viii) nutritional composition and value addition of crops, (ix) food business environment & policy,(x) financial management andfinancing for food industries,(xi) role of NABARD in rural development, (xii) intellectual property rights (IPR) and trademarks, (xiii) project financing and report writing, (xiv) formulation of new product, sensory analysis and acceptability of the developed food items, shelf life and microbial analysis offormulatedfood items, (xv) how to start an enterprise,(xvi) storage of produced crops for use of processing, (xvii) post harvest management of crops, (xviii) entrepreneurial opportunities in food sector,(xix) supply and cold chain management,(xx) food safety and standards,(xxi) food quality analysis and quality control,(xxii) government regulations/guidelines for food sector, (xxiii) banking formalities for new start-up, (xxiv) food licensing, (xxv) role of science and technology, (xxvi) organic farming and its importance, (xxvii) packaging and labelling, (xxviii) success stories of local entrepreneurs and their practical experience, (xxix) maintenance of food processing equipments and industry, (xxx) SWOT analysis, (xxxi) schemes and incentives of different government and non government departments, i.e.,NABARD, DST, DIC, RFC, etc., (xxxii) role of self help groups and their use in entrepreneurship, (xxxiii) capacity building, (xxxiv) unit operations in food processing, (xxxv) food processing, byproduct utilization and waste management, (xxxvi) extrusion technology. (xxxv) probiotic and prebiotic uses of food items,(xxxvi) cost benefit ratio and (xxxvii) demonstration and hands on training of food processing technologies .institution and industrial visits may carried out to understand the working style in actual conditions.

Practical sessions may include the formulation of multiple products by processing of fruits, vegetable, cereal, pulses, nuts and oil seeds.Value added food items such as pickles, murrabas, jam, jelly, candies, cherry, sauces, confectionary goods, papad, bari, mangori, namkeen, sweets, laddu, gulabjamun, rasgulla, juices, squashes, paneer, cakes, biscuits, mathri, instant mixes, capsules, etc. can be prepared by food processing and preservation. These prepared food items can be stored for longer duration.

Financial assistance

Only skills are not enough to establish a new enterprise. It requires a capital which is a big amount for most of the people of grass root level. Thus, they need financial assistance for the purpose. Government of India provides financial assistance (grant-in-aid) through different schemes, i.e., grant-in-aid scheme of ministry of food processing industries (MOFPI). Related schemes or subsidies are given by National Horticulture Board (NHB), National Horticulture Mission (NHM), Small Farmer Agri-Business Consortium (SFAC) assistance to cold storages, Agriculture And Processed Food Products Export Development Authority (APEDA) assistance for cold chain, development commissioner Micro, Small and Medium Enterprises (MSME), venture capital by Small Farmer Agri-Business Consortium (SFAC), venture capital by SIDBI Venture Capital Ltd. (SVLC), funds details of SVLC, Ministry of Micro, Small and Medium Enterprises, Pradhan Mantri Kaushal Vikas Yojana. Other related sections of schemes are Pradhan Mantri Kisan Sampada Yojana, mega food parks, cold chains, Pradhan Mantri Mudra Yojana, make in India initiative, Prime Minister Employment Generation Programme (PMEGP). Mukhyamantri Yuva Swarozgar Loan Yojana (MMYSY), Pradhan Mantri Gramo-Udhyog Yojana and Pradhan Mantri Business Loan Yojana etc. Numerous financial institutions of government and private sectors such as ICICI, IFCI, IDBI, LIC, UTI, SIDBI, NSIC, NBFC, NABARD, UCO, PNB and SBI etc., provide financial assistance to the small-scale industries. These financial institutions are indulged in uplifting of the interest of industries by providing loans, technical assistance and promotional activities. While raising loans from such financial institutions person should file necessary registration on certificate, partnership deed, organization's document, organization audited balance sheet, profit and loss account, original encumbrance certificate approved plans by concerned authorities and photographs of proprietor.

The facilitation of learning by people who can benefit from new information, skills, and attitudes is part of a skill development programme (Kapila, 2015). In this regard, Asif (2000) emphasized that training should be centred on the people' actual requirements. Professional training and skill improvement can assume a significant part for provincial individuals by improving family efficiency, pay, procuring opportunity, employability and so on.These exercises may likewise advance food security and reasonable rural development. Food crops that have been processed may have a higher value and a longer shelf life. Aside from that, the processed product may be accessible all year, and these items might be profitable. Food processing abilities may be taught in youths with the aid of training. They will be trained in confidence development, a variety of food preservation procedures, food handling and bundling. It also generated self-employment opportunities so that individuals can start their own endeavor and can help in upgrading the GDP of our Nation.

References

1. Asif, N. (2000). Utilization of vocational training Sialkot region. An impact study of NRSP-Sialkot. NRSP Monitoring Assessment and Planning Section.
2. Birdar, G., Bhavani, K. (2015). Empowering rural women through small scale food processing unit – an approach. Asian Journal of Home Science. 10(2):462-465.
3. FAO. (2013). Promoting decent employment opportunities for rural youth, available at http://www.fao.org/docrep/018/i2976e/ i2976e.pdf retrieved on 10/12/2016.
4. Fernandez, S., Moldogezeiv, T. (2013). Using employee empowerment to encourage innovative behavior in the public sector. Journal Public Administration Research and Theory. 23(1):155-185.
5. Goel, V.P. (2011). Technical and vocational education and training (TVET) system in India for sustainable development. UNESCO-UNEVOC International Centre for Technical and Vocational Education and Training. Bonn Germany.
6. ILO. (2013). ILO Global employment trends for youth, 2013. Geneva, ILO, available at www.ilo.org/wcmsp5/groups/public/@dgreports/@dcomm/.../wcms_212423.pdf, retrieved on 11.12.2016.
7. Kapila, P. (2015). Impact assessment of skill development programme for rural women in district Ludhiana. Journal of Krishi Vigyan. 3(Special Issue):55-58.
8. Meena, M.S., Singh, R., Meena, H.R., Meena, B.K. (2012). Impact assessment of training on food processing and preservation. Indian Journal of Social Research. 53(2):117-122.
9. Merchant, A. (2008). India –Food Processing Industry. OSEC Business Network: New Delhi.

10. Parvez, S. (2017). A System view time and scope. Journal of Innovation and Entrepreneurship. 6:14.

11. Singh, S.P., Tegegne, F., Ekenem, E. (2012). The food processing industry in India – challenges and opportunities. Journal of Food distribution Research. 43(1):81-89.

12. Tiwari, M., Sanadya, G., Gupta, K. (2017). Skill development among youth under food processing training programmes. International Journal of Current Microbiology and Applied Sciences. 6(8):2607-2610.

13. Tiwari, M., Singh, D.K., Tripathi, N.N., Singh, M. (2016). Post harvest management and food processing. New Delhi: Himanshu Publications.

V

Community Based Social Innovation for Promoting Healthy and Active Aging

Gayatri Prajapati[1] and Khwairakpam Sharmila[2]
[1]Research Scholar and [2]Assistant Professor
Department of Human Development and Family Studies, School of Home Science
Babasaheb Bhimrao Ambedkar University, Lucknow -226025, Uttar Pradesh, India
Email Id: gayatriprajapati250@gmail.com
Khwairakpamsharmila@gmail.com

Abstract

The population of aging age changes the figure of demands on healthcare services. During the adulthood the body is in an exceedingly degenerative process therefore, the physical strength gets reduced. The cognitive and thinking abilities are also become limited. Additionally, the idleness caused by brain makes one feel like loneliness and takes a toll on active social life. Social innovation may be a hopeful viewpoint in the field of aging to deal with these problems and opportunities. It is an orientation towards meeting social needs, challenges and values; the beginning of recent social practices; participants taking part and acceptance; and attainment of both societal and personally avails. Both the developed and developing area's health systems are clashing to fulfill the varied and complicated needs of growingly aging populations. The aim of the innovations is providing health and social safe keeping. Community based social innovations (CBSIs) are a kind of innovation that will assist to handle requirements of senior citizens. This article will examine how innovations help for older adults and what is role of the older adults in this context, and what programs and policies are being run by government of India for older adults. It can help individual's physical and psychological health, enhance their assuredness and self-esteem, and improve their quality of life.

Keywords: Community, Healthcare, Older adults, Program and Policies, Social Innovation.

Introduction

The 2011 Census report shows that the figure of elderly who aged 60 and above in India is around ten crore 40 lakh of which 50 crore 30 lakh are women and 50 crore 10 lakh are Men. UN Population Fund and Help Age India released a report which demonstrates that the elderly population is an estimated to grow to 17.3 crore by 2026. The share and size both of senior citizens have been growing over time. Total percent of elderly population is 8.6 in India 2011. From which 71 percent of older adults exist in non-urban areas as 29 percent is in metropolitan areas, and total 14.2% of older adults are dependent upon other people (vikaspedia, n.d.). Community-based social innovations (CBSIs) is the beginning that endeavors to empower adults to enhance their self-belief in looking after for themselves and their friends, promote their well-being and encourage social solidarity and incorporation. Whereas they must need to enhance care and liberty of older people, and to change healthcare systems, CBSIs need to make better their deeming of optimal traditional and service delivery prototype that connects societies and expansion a spectrum of health and social services (WHO, 2017). Community based social innovations (CBSIs) are one form of innovation which will assist to fulfill requirements of senior citizens. In the context of aging, CBSIs are based on three main principles, which are:

1. Where possible, empowering older adults to care for them.

2. Focus on community encompassment.
3. The improve quality of life in contexts of sickness, incapacity and declining health (Ong et al. 2016).

Organization for economic co-operation and Development 2011 said, "There is social innovation wherever new mechanisms and norms consolidate and improve the well-being of individuals, communities and territories in terms of social inclusion, creation of employment, quality of life" (Sonne L. 2014). Another word of "social innovation is the process of developing and deploying effective solutions to challenging and sometimes systemic social and environmental problems in support of social progress. Social innovation is not the prerogative or privilege of any organizational form or legal structure. Solutions often require the active collaboration of constituents across government, business, and also the nonprofit world". (Soule et.al n.d.) WHO conducted a study on Mental health of older adults in 2017 that the older people which is suffer from dementia are in need of support from physical health, psychological health, social, financial and legal systems for the effective delivery of elderly care. The innovations for ageing population is intentioned for restructuring the existing the services-care, housing, mobility and other important aspects of life- for an elder friendly environment (Herzlinger, 2006). Health services are important areas to be taken care for elderly people. The focus of the innovation is to get convenient, effective, and low cost delivery of health care services to the persons (Howaldt, J. et.al 2010).

Challenges faced by elderly people

Problems faced by elderly included:

Physical problem:

Chronic health issues usually happen in older people age and area unable to perform several of the activities that they could do once. The body of the senior citizens is become more fragile, more drastic, and less flexible. Chronic health related illnesses may cause secondary impairments, or to develop new disease. The physical problems related to the disease can be easily seen. Like as; senior citizens who are suffering from glaucoma may not seem to be physically impaired, but their loss of vision might lead to accidents and falls that may impact their physical health or goodness. They can face walking problem, loss of hearing, unclear vision and Reduction in smell, and suffering from chronic health conditions like; diabetes, cardiovascular, hypertension, arthritis etc. (Senior care n.d.).

Financial Problems:

After 60 year, most of the elderly people become retire Those people who used to work in the private sector do not even get pension, so they have to depend on others, that makes them frustrated. Retirement amount and community safety is limited to those who have employed in the private sector or factory; however, the retired persons are faced with the issue of financial insecurity and isolation. Generally loss of income after retirement from service and the people get insufficient pension which cannot fulfill their own needs, because during this era, medicals checkups, medicines, assistive devices etc. are very expensive. (Prasad R. 2017).

Mental Problems:

Mental problems may cause memory loss, language problem, unable to take decisionand unable to control their emotions. Elderly people who have mild dementia do not need to pay much attention but any type of dementia that is onward and cause serious safety concerns should be noted. A number of cognitive problems are faced by older adults like; they are become in confusion, and some of the time suffering from memory loss called dementia and they don't concentrate any things, forgetting to take medicines on time, and also face language problem.

Emotional Problems:

A decline in health, the loss of life partner, unable to do activities what make them happy or the emotions of unimportance are all problems that may cause to experience emotional problems. Depression, social distance, isolation, change in personality such as; irritable, angry, unstable emotions, moody etc., lack of interest in various activities etc. are some of the emotional problem which is faced by elderly (Senior care n.d.).

Social innovation services for older adults

1. HELPAGE INDIA:

HelpAge India founded in 1978, it is an Indian organization focused on the distress of older adults, and its mission is "to work for the cause and care of underprivileged older persons and to make better their quality of life". This service investigates their requirement with the State and Central governments, such as; many types of services and Retirement amount, quality health care, taking steps against person which exploit with Elder, and any other programs at the societal, state and national level. It runs many healthcare programs for senior citizens. The purpose of this organization served underprivileged elderly holistically, so that they can lead an active, respectful & good health life (Wikipedia n.d.). HelpAge's focus has moved from Welfare to Development over the years. It provides happiness of elderly through several agecare intervention programs such as; Mobile healthcare program which is one of the largest mobile healthcare units in the country which is providing free healthcare services to destitute older adults (HelpAge India 2021).

Starting from restoration of vision, geriatric physiotherapy, to treat musculoskeletal diseases and make Elderly's daily living easier, HelpAge provide essentials requirements and help to keep their daily lives, Palliative care services (India), mobile hospital services (e.g., Smile on Wheels, India), Elder Helplines and day care centers are programs servicing the needs of underprivileged older people. (Wikipedia n.d. para.1 & KV. S et.al 2012)

2. AGEWELL FOUNDATION:

Agewell Foundation is a non-profit NGO working since 1999 for the welfare and empowerment of older people in India (Agewell Foundation 2011 para.1). This Foundation is committed to making a coordinated effort with compassion and understanding to change social attitudes towards seniors. There is an effort to build infrastructure to empower every elderly. Agewell has been set up to initiate better interactions between generations. The main aim of this foundation is; changing perceptions about aging, taking steps towards a favorable environment for elderly people, developing a moral sense and social responsibility towards senior citizens, advocating for the requirements and rights of senior citizens wherever necessary To help (Agewell Foundation 2009).

3. *SPARSH:*

Sparsh stands of "**Social Innovation programme for Products: Affordable & Relevant to Societal Health.**" The program has been launched by BIRAC under the Department of Biotechnology, Ministry of Science and Technology and Government of India. The objectives of this program for promote the development of new solutions to the most pressing community trouble of society. The plan will tackle general social problems and introduce innovative thinks for wider transformation. The plan purposes to think about suggestion and novations that better the healthcare of people & promote inexpensive material for development in the local field. The purpose of this plan intends to make a pool of social inventors in the biotech sector which is recognize distinct requirements and gaps in healthcare. The Social inventors will be given technical & economical help to develop commercial-founded solutions that have the probable to introduce cost-efficient healthcare success, particularly to sensitive individuals (India science, Technology & innovation 2021).

4. *NASSCOM Social Innovation Forum (NSIF):*

The National Association of Software and Service Companies "(NASSCOM) Social Innovation Forum (NSIF)" is a "Take for Good" platform aimed at addressing technology-based innovation for pyramid (BoP) population base by evolving solutions to bridge gaps in key growth areas and promote inclusive development. The foundation attracted over one thousand new projects from Non-government organizations, private sector, social enterprises, governments, individuals and students. In which some of the project are Elderly's related like as; (NASSCOM Foundtion 2021).

4. a) *Assistive Devices:*

Through this project, elderly and disabled people are provided with assistive technology and expensive treatment. Some service is included like; wearable safety devices, technologies and low cost assistive devices those make an enabling atmosphere for individuals with inabilities and make daily activities handy. e.g.; climbing the vehicle walking and navigation, talk with someone, studying writing and more (NASSCOM Foundtion 2021). By ensuring access to technology and information, the basic concept of Assistive technology is to make an elder friendly environment by assisting them in their daily life. It helps the elders to maintain independence, assists in healthcare services, manage the loneliness, make healthy environment in own house, access to information, helps in increased social interaction, etc. (Gamberiniet. al, 2006).

4. b) Healthcare sanitation:

In this project, ensuring a healthy life and improving their healthcare for every persons of all ages is important for perpetual development. Over seventy percent population living in a non-urban area and living below the poverty line, access of quality Medicare remains a clash for most of India's population. Past few years, the immense capability of Information and Communication Technology has been used to digitize healthcare to public (NASSCOM Foundtion 2021). The different sets of ideas linked to technology and elderly care. It starts with tele-health care that can be useful to get heath care advices and maintain a contact with the elderly person and the health care specialist (Gamberiniet. al, 2006).

Welfare program and scheme for senior citizen in India

1.) The National Programme for Health Care of the Elderly (NPHCE):

"National Policy on Older Persons" as well as the State's obligation under the "Maintenance & Welfare of Parents & Senior Citizens Act 2007", the Ministry of Health & Family Welfare founded the "National Programme for the Health Care of Elderly" (NPHCE) in 2010, in eleventh Plan period, to resolve many health concerns of older adults (National health Mission 2021). The program envisages providing promotional, preventive, and therapeutic & rehabilitation services for the seniors in many governments health facilities. The category of services would comprise health promotion, precautionary services; prognostic and management of old age health issue, day care services, rehabilitation services and nursing as required. The zone would be connected to regional geriatric centers to provide care of tertiary level (National Health Programme 2015). Through the physiotherapy unit at Chronic Health Center, District Hospital and Regional Geriatrics Center levels, by arranging therapeutic modalities such as medical practice, training in Activities of Daily Living (ADL) and cure of pain and swelling, for which essential infrastructure, medicine and devices are given that these problems (National Health Mission 2021).

2. *National Action Plan for Welfare of Senior Citizens (NAPSrC):*

It is an umbrella scheme for senior citizens, which was launched in 2020 by the Government of India, Ministry of Social Justice and Empowerment, Department of Social Justice and Empowerment. The top four types of requirements for senior citizens gives by this scheme such as; *Meal, Economic security Medicare and connect with human / life of dignity.* This program has been started with awareness generation and sensitization of the community and also included aspects of safety and wellbeing of the older people. To make an atmosphere where every person can live a dignity's life, age and dignity, with expertise in concrete and coordinated action on the extant and prominent needs of seniors (Social justice 2021). There are mainly two types of programs under this scheme which provide welfare for senior citizens:

2. a) *Integrated Programme for Senior Citizens (IPSrC):*

This scheme was also known as "Integrated Programme for Older Persons (IPOP)." (Govtempdiary 2020). Under this scheme, financial help up to ninety percent of the project value is granted to Governments/ Union Territory Administrations (UT)/ Panchayati Raj Institutions/ Local bodies; Non Governmental/ Voluntary Organizations for maintenance of Senior Citizens Homes which is called Old Age Homes/ Continuous Care Homes, Mobile Medicare Units (MMU), physiotherapy clinics for senior citizens etc., (Government of India 2018). This scheme's purpose is to enhance their wellbeing and quality of life of the older adults and encouraging productive and active aging by giving fundamental facilities like: asylum, meal, and Medicare and recreation opportunities to older persons and providing support to capacity (Vikaspedia 2021).

2. b) *State Action Plan for Senior Citizens (SAPSrC):*

MWPSC Act 2007, (The Maintenance and Welfare of Parents & Senior Citizens) states that health care for seniors will be provided by the State Governments. The primary objective of this programs is to provide recognition and opportunities for seniors to contribute and thus to feel useful to community, to promote healthcare and quality of life of seniors, to encourage productive and active aging. Many more programs are being run under this program such as; To Maintain of Mobile Medicare Unit (MMU), physiotherapy clinics, and construction of a pool of trained old age cares for seniors, and for cataracts to achieve the vision of a cataract-free state Special campaign for cataract surgery for senior citizens (Government of India 2021).

3. *Rashtriya Vayoshri Yojana:*

This Yojana was founded on 2017, 01 April and is under the administrative control of the Ministry of Social Justice and Empowerment (Govtempdiary 2020). It is a **central sector scheme** funded by the **Senior Citizen Welfare Fund** which was announced in 2016 (Dristi 2020). The scheme aims for senior citizens who belong to the BPL (below poverty line) category and are affected by any age related disability or weakness like; hearing problem, nearsighted or farsighted, teeth weakening, and locomotor disability will be provided assistive-living devices that can restore nearly normal to their physical functions, overcoming manifest disability / weakness. The scheme is expected to benefit all older people across the country (Rastriya Vayoshri Yojana 2019). Under the scheme, daily living equipment such as canes, crutches, walkers, wheelchairs, tripod / quad pods, hearing device, tricycle artificial Dentures, eyeglasses etc. are endowed free of cost which seniors whose needed it.

4. *National Social Assistance Programme:*

This program was started on August 15, 1959 (Vikaspedia 2021). It is a welfare program administered by the Ministry of Rural Development. This program is being enforced in urban as well as rural areas (NSAP 2011). NSAP is a social security / social welfare program that apply to elderly people, disabled persons, widows, whose belonging to BPL category (Gconnect 2019).

Currently NSAP includes some sub-scheme for seniors, that is;

4. a) *Indira Gandhi National Old Age Pension Scheme (IGNOAPS):*

Individuals who belonging to below poverty line (BPL) family. Under this scheme, central assistance will give persons whose aged 60-79 years Rs. 200/ month and five hundred rupees /month to individual aged eighty years or above. The scheme is executed by the States / Union Territories. Under the schemes, identified of receiver, acceptance and dispersal of benefits are completed by the government (Gconnect 2019).

4. b) *Indira Gandhi National Widow Pension Scheme (IGNWPS):*

In this scheme, three hundred rupees per month given 40 years age widow women and after obtaining the age of eighty years, its amount is increased to Rs 500 / - per month (SSWCD 2021). Under this scheme widows who are living below the poverty line will get Rs. 300/- every month until their death. Contribution to the scheme is made to support the Central Government, State Government, to increase the livelihood of widows living in rural areas to confirm the widows living below poverty line receive financial allowances and benefits from the government (Indiafilling 2021).

4. c) *Indira Gandhi National Disability Pension Scheme (IGNDPS):*

The appropriate age for this scheme is eighteen years and 18+ & the inability/ infirmity level should be eighty percent. The pension amount is three hundred rupees every month and after getting the age of eighty years, the identified individuals will get Rs five hundred every month. Midgets will also be admissible for this grant (Vikaspedia 2021).

4. d) *Annapurna:*

In this scheme, 10 kg of grain is given to each beneficiary per month.The scheme purpose to provide Meal security to cater to the needs of appropriate older adults whose are not covered under IGNOAPS (Vikaspedia 2021 NSAP).

5. Medical facilities for Senior Citizens:

The AYUSH Ministry has been providing the following facilities to older adults such as; Under Yoga and Naturopathy, free counseling and yoga therapy, OPD is being provided in various government hospitals, free yoga training and other programs like; Yoga Therapy Program, Health Promotion Program, Therapy Session, Individual Yoga, Week of the day Yoga Training Program, Monthly Diagnostic workshop of Yoga therapy etc. The main purpose of this plan is to make the elderly free from disease and improve their wellbeing of them so that they can lead a quality life (Gconnect 2019).

Conclusion

As people get older they become dependent on others and they have to face many more problems like physical, psychological, financial etc. To overcome all this, social innovation and the schemes and programs run by the government are proving to be very helpful for the elderly. The health benefits are usually psychosocial for older people and communities. The community based social innovation (CBSI) activities provided them a means of interacting with peers, helping, and living active lifestyles. Thereby helping beneficiaries keep away from social isolation and loneliness that can benefit mental. CBSIs can facilitate contributions to people-centric services by empowering and engaging society and assisting to create social networks to adherence older individuals. Some Community Based Social Innovations have an also impact on physical health. It empowers older people to take care of themselves and their peers, enriching their well-being and quality of life, and improve their self-efficacy in promoting social adjustment and inclusiveness.

References

1. Agewell Foundation (2011) Retrieved from https://www.agewellfoundation.org/
2. Agewell Foundation (2009). Agewell Foundation, India. Retrieved from https://www.slideshare.net/agewellfoundation/agewell-foundation

3. Dristi (2020). Rashtriya Vayoshri Yojana. Retrieved from https://www.drishtiias.com/daily-updates/daily-news-analysis/rashtriya-vayoshri-yojana

4. Govtempdiary (2020). Welefare schemes & Programmes for senior citizens. Available here https://www.govtempdiary.com/2019/05/schemes-programmes-for-welfare-of-senior-citizens/56642

5. GovernmentofIndia(2018).Availableherehttp://164.100.24.220/loksabhaquestions/annex/15/AU969.pdf

6. Government of India (2021). Atal vayo abhyuday yojna (AVYAY). available here http://socialjustice.nic.in/writereaddata/UploadFile/AVYAY%20pdf.pdf

7. Gconnect (2019). Schemes and programmes for welfare of senior citizens. Available here https://www.gconnect.in/news/schemes-programmes-welfare-senior-citizens.html

8. Gamberini et. al, (2006). Cognition, technology and games for the elderly: An introduction to ELDERGAMES Project, PsychNology Journal Volume 4, Number 3, pp. 285 -308.

9. Howaldt, J., Schwarz, M., Henning K. & Hees F. (2010). Social Innovation: Concepts, research fields, and international trends, IMA/ZLW & IfU, IMO International Monitoring (Vol 5)

10. Herzlinger, (2006). Why innovation in healthcare is so hard, Harvard business review 84(5):58-66, 156. Retrieved April 13, 2020 from https://hbr.org/2006/05/why-innovation-in-health-care-is-so-hard

11. HelpAge India (2021). HelpAge India, Fighting isolation, poverty, neglect. Retrieved from https://www.helpageindia.org/

12. India filling (2021). Indira Gandhi national widow scheme, retrieved from indiafilings.com/learn/indira-gandhi-national-widow-pension-scheme/

13. India science, Technology & innovation (2021). Social Innovation Programme For Products: Affordable & Relevant To Societal Health (SPARSH) Retrieved from https://www.indiascienceandtechnology.gov.in/funding-opportunities/startups/social-innovation-programme-products-affordable-relevant-societal

14. K.V.S; RM.C & Manzoor R. (2012) Social Innovation as an instrument for productive and self reliant ageing. Published in Pacific Business Review International; vol. 5(6)

15. National Health Programme (2015). National program for health care elderly (NPHCE). Available here https://www.nhp.gov.in/national-

program-of-health-care-for-the-elderlyn

16. National Health Mission (2021). National Programme for Healthcare of Elderly (NPHCE). Retrieved from https://nhm.gov.in/index1.php?lang=1&level=2&sublinkid=1046&lid=605

17. NSAP (2011). National social assistance programme. Retrieved from https://nsap.nic.in/circular.do?method=aboutus

18. NASSCOM Foundtion (2021). Retrieved from https://nasscomfoundation.org/nsif/

19. Ong, P., L. Garcon & A. Ross. 2016. 'First Expert Consultation on Community-Based Social Innovations that Support Older People in Low- and Middle-Income Countries.' 14–15 July 2015, Kobe, Japan. Geneva, World Health Organization.

20. Prasad R. (2017). Problems of senior citizens in India. Published by international journal of humanities and social science research; vol 3; (1) p.n. 35-37

21. Rastriya Vayoshri Yojana (2019). Available here https://www.india.gov.in/spotlight/rashtriya-vayoshri-yojana

22. Senior care (n.d.). Senior care. Available here https://www.seniorcare.org/elder-care/

23. Social justice (2021). National Action Plan for Welfare of Senior Citizens (NAPWSrC). Retrieved from http://socialjustice.nic.in/writereaddata/UploadFile/NAPSrC.pdf

24. Sonne L. (2014), social innovation in India. Retrieved from https://www.merit.unu.edu/wp-content/docs/25years/presentations/sonne.pdf

25. Soule A.S., Malhotra N., Clavier B., (n.d.) defining social innovation. Retrieved from https://www.gsb.stanford.edu/faculty-research/centers-initiatives/csi/defining-social-innovation

26. SSWCD (2021). Indira Gandhi national widow scheme (IGNWPS). Retrieved from https://sswcd.punjab.gov.in/en/indira-gandhi-national-widow-pension-scheme-ignwps-0

27. Vikaspedia (2021). Schemes for senior citizens. Retrieved from https://vikaspedia.in/social-welfare/senior-citizens-welfare/schemes

28. Vikaspedia (2021). National social assistance program (NSAP). Retrieved from https://vikaspedia.in/social-welfare/rural-poverty-alleviation-1/schemes/national-social-assistance-programme

29. Vikaspedia (n.d). Senior citizens status in India. Retrieved April 24, 2021 from https://vikaspedia.in/social-welfare/senior-citizens-welfare/senior-

citizens-status-in india

30. WHO (2017). Understanding community based social innovation for healthy ageing. Retrieved fromhttps://extranet.who.int/kobe_centre/sites/default/files/pdf/WHO%20CBSI%20Main%20Report_FINAL.pdf

31. Wikipedia (n.d). HelpAgeIndia. Retrieved April 27, 2021 from https://en.wikipedia.org/wiki/HelpAge_India

VI

Role of Women in Different Aspects of Development

Nidhi[1] and Dr. Neetu Singh[2]
[1]Research scholar and [2]Associate Professor
Department of Human Development and Family Studies,
School of Home Science Babasaheb Bhimrao Ambedkar (A Central) University
Lucknow -226025, Uttar Pradesh, India
Email Id: nidhigautam451@gamil.com

Abstract

Women are the primary sources of income for themselves and their families. When women become economically, socially and politically empowered, they benefit for the broader community and women have two jobs, around the home and outside. This implies that women have an important contribution to make to the healthy socioeconomic development of all countries but women are constantly deprived of this opportunity due to the nature of our societal organization and the cultural structure that makes the maintenance of the status quo more convenient for men. Women's contribution to the successful transition from pre-literacy to literacy in a society, from a relatively self-reliant community to a member of a nation mixed with a global economy, too little attention has been paid by social scientists and decision-makers. The role of women in development countries, as researched in this module was considered to be the most important factor in generating and supporting social change in the long run. Ladies are peasants and food suppliers, businessmen and shopkeepers, housekeepers, mothers, career and support workers and play numerous other roles such as community leaders, activist, and role models. In nearly every place in the world and into all conceivable dimension of socio-economic life, there are many barriers for women to lead healthy and fulfilling lives. They have been denied access to educational opportunities as a result of beliefs about the limitations of their social roles and responsibilities to the performance of their duties, and taking care of infant & other reproduction activities where little or no education is needed. The aim of such subject to evaluate women's role in development from a variety of perspectives.

Keywords:*Community Development, Economic Development, Empowered, Social Development, Women.*

Introduction

In today's world, the role and the status of women has disappeared radically transformed as a result of globalization and commercialization in India but only 33% of women work in economic employment due to women are not making decisions for economic activity and they still financially dependent on their parents.[Alam, S.]The women's empowerment and autonomy and improved political, social, economic and health outcomes situation are of great importance objectives in their own right. Moreover, it is crucial for achieving sustainable development. Education is among the most important ways to empower women who have the necessary knowledge, skills and self-confidence for full participation in the course of development. Four decades ago, the Universal Declaration of Human Rights said so "every person has the right to education".[UNFPA] The proposed Women's Reserves Act [Constitution Act (108th Amendment) was passed by the Rajya Sabha (Executive Chamber of the Parliament of India) on 9[th]March, 2010[Wikigender]According to the Inter parliamentary Union, in 2018, only 24% of MPs were women.[Geetika Dang]

1. Role of Women in Different aspect of Development

1. a Women as providers of educators

The commitment made by ladies to the change from pre-educated to proficient society is likewise irrefutable. Fundamental training is vital for a country's ability to build up and meet maintainable improvement objectives.[Michele gran] Women's role in the education system can have an important role in society.[Nousheen Zeeshan]

Savitri Phule became the first teacher at India's first girls' school. She has worked her whole life for the dignity of the lives of the oppressed-caste persons and women. Her leadership has marked the grand entrance by women to the public space of contemporary India. Savitribai set up an instructive society which opened more schools for young ladies and ladies of all classes in the encompassing towns. She additionally established Mahila Seva Mandal to show ladies their privileges, pride and social issues in 1952.Savitri Phule is the mother of India's feminism, and contributions to women education among her struggles for oppression and women leave a permanent mark on the story.[Anureet]

Ramabai Ranade was the leading women's rights activist and pioneer of the modern women's movement. For the past 25 years, she has worked vigorously on women's education, legal rights, equality of status and general awareness. She struggled with the child marriage system and also founded the women's institution called Seva Sadan in Bombay & Pune, which was followed by thousands of women. She set up a branch of Arya Mahila Samaj in the city and the Hindu Ladies Social & Literary Club in Mumbai. Similarly, she started several courses to train women in languages, general knowledge, sewing and handicrafts. On that front, women have done a lot of work in education and they're doing more and they're going to do more.[MeMumbai]

1.b Women as caretaker

Caregivers, particularly women, play a vital role, like taking care of her family, taking care of everyone she 'left behind' herself. Ladies guardians who were surrendered to the social assumption that they would verifiably do the consideration giving work anticipated response past the typical acknowledgment of being viewed as a 'decent' parental figure by the family, or the expectation of otherworldly rewards.[Ugargol,et all]Mother Mary Teresa Bojaxhiu honored in the Catholic Church as St Teresa of Calcutt. She began minister work with the poor in 1948 and established a school in Motijhil, Kolkata, prior to beginning to take care of poor people and yearning. Toward the start of 1949 Teresa was participated in her work by a gathering of young ladies, and established the framework for another strict local area helping the "least fortunate among poor people". By blood, I am Albanian, by citizenship, an Indian, by faith, I am a Catholic nun, as to my calling, I belong to the world, as to my heart, I belong entirely to the Heart of Jesus," said Teresa. Aarticulate speaker of 5accents– Albanian, Bengali, Serbian, Hindi & English- she occasionally travelled outside India on humanitarian grounds.[Wikipedia]

1.c Women as economic developer

To awaken individuals, ladies should be stirred. At the point when she moves, the family moves, the town moves, the country moves"- Pandit Jawaharlal Nehru. Country ladies' make up the biggest useful workforce in the economy of most of non-industrial nations, including India. They often manage more complex housework and have a variety of subsistence strategies on a daily basis. They for the most part doing numerous works including creating horticultural yields, tending creatures, planning food, functioning as a work in the rural field for the wages, gathering fuel and water, washing garments, participate in advertising, raising the kids and caring the relatives and generally keeping up with the entire house. They work number of labor-intensive jobs in the agricultural field like weeding, hoeing, grass cutting, picking, cotton stick collection, plucking vegetables and plucking sunflowers, separating of seeds from fiber, keeping of livestock etc. In home relating to the production like milking, preparation of ghee, curd, chesses etc. As per Swaminathan, a few antiquarians accept that it is the one who initially tamed the developed plants and who started the craftsmanship and study of agribusiness in them. While men went out chasing looking for food, ladies began gathering seeds from the local vegetation and started developing those of interest according to the perspective of food, feed, fssodder, fiber and fuel.[Archana Behera]

1.d Women as homemakers

Ladies' work is still ineffectively comprehended and officially sloppy in spite of the way that ladies' commitments to the family are essential; much of the time ladies are providers and work longer hours.[Sidh, S. N.et al]Ladies are a lady in each general public makes a significant commitment to building a solid and sound country. They effectively partake in homegrown and useful exercises, and they assume the double duty of sustenance, wellbeing and family training inside and outside the family, essentially on family cultivates. [Jabeen, S] It assumes a vital part in the arrangement and administration of suppers, choice and support of apparel, brightening, outfitting and upkeep of the house. The woman acts as a humble family income administrator. It always prefers to come up with a surplus budget rather than a deficit budget. The entire burden of procreation and a larger part of the education of children is borne by the women in the home. Mother is the primary instructor of the youngster, gives the social inheritance to the kid and organizes the home and exercises to guarantee that each individual from the family has sufficient food, satisfactory rest and entertainment.[Shauni]

1.e Women as entreprenurs

The rise of ladies business visionaries and their commitment to the country's economy is obviously apparent in India. The quantity of female business visionaries has grown up over the long run, particularly during the 1990s. Ladies business people ought to be praised for their expanded utilization of current advancements, expanded speculation, discovering a specialty in the fare market, making significant positions for other people, and set up the pattern for different ladies business people in the coordinated area. Female business people make new positions for themselves and for other people, and furthermore in light of the fact that they are extraordinary. They give society various arrangements, like administration, association and answers for business issues, just as working business openings.[Kumar, S].]In this speedy world, ladies business people assume a significant part in the worldwide quest for manageable financial turn of events and social turn of events. In India, while ladies have assumed a vital part in the general public, their pioneering capacity has not been as expected tapped because of the lower status of ladies in the general public.[Ambiga, S., & Ramasamy, M]At the end of the day, ladies business people are frequently portrayed as survivalists and rule low-gifted, low-capital and regularly casual and miniature business organizations. They will in general zero in on organizations that seek after their public jobs, similar to the help area and contribute similarly to the improvement of adjusted provincial turn of events and the improvement of the way of life in the country. they are the main entertainers who advance the way of life of society.[G.Malyadri, D. G. M.]

1.f Women as activist

For the past decade, there has been a resurgence of women's activism; The complacency of the post-independence period was replaced by an awareness of women's oppression, indignation and action.[Everett, J.]

Indian social lobbyist who was the primary female individual from the Indian Police Service (IPS) and who assumed a critical part in the presentation of jail change in India. She has additionally established two volunteer non-legislative associations, Navjyoti (1988) and India Vision Foundation (1994), both made to oversee essential instruction and grown-up education projects and business preparing and guiding administrations for ladies, just as substance misuse restoration administrations for detainees.[Encyclopaedia Britannica]

Sarojini Naidu was a political lobbyist, women's activist, poetess and the principal Indian lady to be leader of the Indian National Congress and become legislative head of the Indian state. She was in some cases called "the Nightingale of India".[Encyclopaedia Britannica]

1.g Women as leader

Regardless of a solid male centric culture, it is somewhat incomprehensible that India has created incalculable ladies pioneers throughout the years at both the public and hierarchical levels. Agent Indian ladies pioneers who have served in key public, political, and corporate administrative roles incorporate Indira Gandhi, the primary female Prime Minister of India; Pratibha Patil, the principal female President of India; Indira Nooyi, the main lady and first individual of Indian plummet to lead Pepsi Co.; and Chitra Ramakrishna, the main lady CEO of the National Stock Exchange, India's driving stock trade. These ladies chiefs keep on being good examples for all hopeful youthful Indian ladies as they have scaled the highest point of their professions and left their engraving on the fresher age of ladies pioneers. [Chaudhuri, S., Park, S., & Kim, S]

1.h Women as pride of nation

Kalpana Chawla's first opportunity to fly in space in November 1997, on board the space transport 16793-first-space-transport Columbia on flight STS-87.[Nola Taylor Redd]To respect it, NASA has named one of its spaceships Kalpana Chawla.[Jashodhara Mukherjee]

Equity M Fathima Beevi is the main lady to be named an appointed authority of the Supreme Court of India. She was likewise the main Muslim lady in the predominant legal framework and the primary lady to fill in as a Supreme Court judge in an Asian country.Her appointment to the Supreme Court opened the door to careers in a male-dominated judicial system.[Khushi Agarwal]

Arati Saha turned into Asia's first lady to swim across the English Channel in 1959. She swam for 16 hours and 20 minutes, batting intense waves and covered 42 miles. After showing up at the English coast, she raised the Indian banner. She was the main Indian competitor to get the Padma Shri Award.[Khushi Agarwal]

Sarla Thakral was the first female Indian to fly in the air.She obtained a Class A licence after 1,000 hours of flying, making history because she was the first to do so.[Saumya]

Similarly, in many other fields also women participated enthusiastically and contributed, which also made the country proud and will continue to do so.

Importance of women in every field

In India, the job of ladies relies upon an assortment of factors like instructive status, societal position and geographic status. Including ladies in the financial advancement of the nation is called engaging ladies. Ladies' strengthening is characterized as the improvement of ladies' capacity to get to the segments of progress, specifically wellbeing, instruction, pay openings, rights and political interest. In India, they assume a double part in delivering labor and products just as their homegrown undertakings, spouses and moms, however their commitment to monetary advancement has been dismissed. The most frequently cited problems were health, malnutrition, repeated reproduction and education, etc. In order to increase women's participation in economic development, women must be provided with the following services: preparing for income creating exercises, simple admittance to low-intrigue advances, and family arranging administrations to restrict reproduction. Putting the ladies at the core of the worldwide policymaking will go far towards understanding the United Nations 2030 Agenda objective of accomplishing sex fairness and engaging all ladies and young ladies. Exchange and Women's Economic Empowerment is that actions pointed toward engaging ladies financially occur gradually and not methodically. Ladies are no less qualified for send out and other well-paying positions; they regularly need admittance to data, money and innovation.[Angala Eswari, G.]

The WID & WAD approaches both identify women as distinct and a separate group in a process to improve their socio-economic conditions were then turned to the Gender and Development Approach (DAG) to overcome certain limitations of those earlier approaches. Women participation in development interventions is one of the prerequisites for the improvement of their socioeconomic condition. It was found that where appropriate mechanisms for women's participation exist, women play a vital role in decision-making, implementation, monitoring and evaluation of development interventions.[Devi, T.]

Ladies of various classes (standings or religions) have totally different jobs and in this way partake in an alternate status corresponding to each other. In conventional India, addressed by the two Hindus and Muslims, a lady had a particularly second rate credited status that was put together not with respect to singular capacity, ability and achievement yet on acquired situations in the general public. She was just viewed as an individual from a family or gathering in the job of a little girl, companion or mother and she has to a great extent denied her part as an individual with a character, yearning or right of her own.[Ghosh R. N., & Roy, K. C]

Ladies are makers of food (adding to rural creation, the general upkeep of the climate and food security); they are money managers and dealers (40% of the world's workforce is female, also casual work at home, on the land, on the work market, and so forth); they are heads of families (the majority of whom are probably going to likewise make some full memories work, just as focusing on kids, older or wiped out family members); they are moms, assistants and backing workers(most regularly in non-industrial nations this is a willful activity); and they are grassroots pioneers, activists, and job models(as an outcome of their job in the public eye as moms, guardians and backing laborers).[Ciara Regan]

Conclusion

Women are the country's trailblazers of the nation; they are the key to sustainable development and quality of life in the family. Women have a variety of roles in the family: wife, leader, administrator, manager of family income and, well, not the least, the mother. Furthermore, it is women who have underpinned the growth of society and shaped the future of nations. At the same time, she plays the role of wife, partner, organizer, administrator, director, re-designer, fundraiser, economist, mother, discipline, teacher, health worker, artist and queen in the family.Beyond this, they play a key role in the socioeconomic development of society.They have created groups, co-operative societies and unions that have spoken out and, have also contributed to the socio-economic development of their communities in particular in the area of poverty reduction and the delivery of social and religious services. Women must be empowered and facilitated, so that their productivity may be increased and country can progress.

References

1. Alam, S. (2020). *Performance of Women ' S Work Contribution in an Indian Economy*. Sambodhi ugc care journal. 43(4)
2. UNFPA (2018). https://www.unfpa.org/resources/issue-7-women-empowerment
3. Wikigender(2021). India: the women's reservation bill https://www.wikigender.org/wiki/india-the-womens-reservation-bill/
4. Geetika Dang (2019). Women's Reservation Bill: what can India learn from other countries?https://www.brookings.edu/blog/up-front/2019/10/18/womens-reservation-bill-what-can-india-learn-from-other-countries/
5. Michele gran (2019). The global role of women- caretakers, conscience, farmers, educatiors and enterpreneurs. https://globalvolunteers.org/global-role-of-women/

6. Nousheen Zeeshan. Women's Role in Education in India https://womennow.in/womens-role-education-india/

7. Anureet (2020). The fierce women who paved the way for women's education in India. https://www.shethepeople.tv/home-top-video/womens-education-india-pioneers-savitribai-phule-fatima-sheikh-anutai-wagh/

8. MeMumbai(2021). Ramabai Ranade (25 January 1863-1924). https://memumbai.com/ramabai-ranade/

9. Ugargol, A. P., Bailey, A., Ugargol, A. P., & Bailey, A. (2018). Family caregiving for older adults: gendered roles and caregiver burden in emigrant households of. *Asian Population Studies, 14*(2), 194–210. https://doi.org/10.1080/17441730.2017.1412593

10. Wikipedia (2021). https://en.wikipedia.org/wiki/Mother_Teresa

11. *Archana Behera,* (2019). *RURAL WOMEN AND AGRICULTURAL DEVELOPMENT IN INDIA; international journal of development in india09(12), 32757–32762.*

12. Sidh, S. N., Basu, &sharmisthaS. (2011). Women's contribution to household food and economic security: A study in the Garhwal Himalayas, India. *Mountain Research and Development, 31*(2), 102–111. https://doi.org/10.1659/MRD-JOURNAL-D-10-00010.1

13. Jabeen, S., Haq, S., Jameel, A., Hussain, A., Asif, M., Hwang, J., & Jabeen, A. (2020). Impacts of rural women's traditional economic activities on household economy: Changing economic contributions through empowered women in rural Pakistan. *Sustainability (Switzerland), 12*(7), 1–23. https://doi.org/10.3390/su12072731

14. Shauni. Role of Women in the Family and Society.https://www.yourarticlelibrary.com/family/role-of-women-in-the-family-and-society/47638

15. Kumar, S. (2019). A Review on Women's Role in Economic Development in India. *SSRN Electronic Journal, 2*(March), 6(2), 9–13. https://doi.org/10.2139/ssrn.3563454

16. Ambiga, S., & Ramasamy, M. (2013). Women entrepreneurship development in India. *JurnalTeknologi (Sciences and Engineering), 64*(3), 167–170. https://doi.org/10.11113/jt.v64.2289

17. G.Malyadri, D. G. M. (2012). Role of women Entrepreneurs in the Economic Development of India. *Paripex - Indian Journal Of Research, 3*(3), 104–105.

18. Everett, J. (2016). The Upsurge of Women's Activism in India. 7(2), 18–26. https://sci-hub.do/https://doi.org/10.2307/3346281

19. Encyclopaedia Britannica (2021). Kiran Bedi Indian activist.https://www.britannica.com/biography/Kiran-Bedi

20. Encyclopaedia Britannica (2021). Sarojini Naidu Indian writer and political leader https://www.britannica.com/biography/Sarojini-Naidu

21. Chaudhuri, S., Park, S., & Kim, S. (2019). *The Changing Landscape of Women ' s Leadership in India and Korea From Cultural and Generational Perspectives*, 18(1), 16-46https://doi.org/10.1177/1534484318809753

22. Nola Taylor Redd (2017). Kalpna chawla: biography & Columbia disaster.https://www.space.com/17056-kalpana-chawla-biography.html

23. Jashodhara Mukherjee (2020). 17 Years After Kalpana Chawla's Death, Her Father Opens Up About Her Dream.https://www.news18.com/news/buzz/17-years-after-kalpana-chawlas-death-her-father-opens-up-about-her-dream-2941149.html

24. Khushi Agarwal (2019). Justice Fatima Beevi: The First Indian Women To Become A Supreme court Justice. https://feminisminindia.com/2019/09/13/justice-fathima-beevi-first-indian-woman-supreme-court-justice/

25. Mark Frost (2014).https://www.channelswimmingdover.org.uk/content/swimmer/saha-arati

26. Saumya(2019). Meet Sarla Thakral, India's first women to fly a plane. https://www.shethepeople.tv/home-top-video/meet-sarla-thakral-indias-first-woman-to-fly-a-plane/ Saumya (2019

27. Angala Eswari, G. (2019). A Study on Role of Women in Economic Development in India. *Shanlax International Journal of Economics*, 7(4), 41–45. https://doi.org/10.34293/economics.v7i4.619

28. Devi, T. (2019). Role of women in rural development. *International Journal of Advanced Science and Technology*, 28(12), 542–544. https://doi.org/10.2307/3517067

29. Ghosh R. N., & Roy, K. C. (1997). The changing status of women in India: impact of urbanization and development. *International Journal of Social Economics*, 24(7–9), 902–917. https://doi.org/10.1108/03068299710178937

30. Ciara Regan (2012). Women & Developmenthttps://developmenteducation.ie/feature/women-development/

VII

Women Collectives lead the Process: Understanding how women are making local communities sensitive to Nutrition needs of women and Adolescent girls

Dr. Sarita Anand[1] and Ms. Ankita Kumari[2]
[1]Associate Professor and [2]Scholar
Department of Development Communication and Extension, Lady Irwin College
Email Id: sarita.anand@lic.du.ac.in

Abstract

Women comprise about 49.6% of the total world population. Constituting almost half of the population this makes their participation a crucial factor in catalyzing the development process. Mobilizing women to participate and take initiatives, has proven to be a promising approach towards inclusive development. Women's self-help groups have been considered as instruments for empowering women by enhancing their economic contribution to the family. However, women's participation yield benefit to them and their families which go far beyond just the economic gains. These gains may be more subtle and gradual like getting voice heard and their enhancing agency within the family and community. Their empowerment in terms of personal and social growth has direct effect on their sense of freedom, self-esteem, self-identity, and capacity to make informed choices. Moreover, learning from engagement in one initiative gets permeated into all aspects of women's livels and helps to break the vicious cycle of gender inequality. A synergy between the large government supported programmes which are flexible to accommodate local needs and cultural nuances seem to work better for women. Developing more gender inclusive programmes is imminent for expanding women's participation. SHGs can be leveraged as platforms to initiate behavior change and improving health and nutrition outcomes, can be one of the focus areas in addition to economic and political benefits. The paper examines the benefits and challenges of participation and leadership roles being taken up by women in a tribal setting for implementing a Gender and Nutrition Support initiative.

Keywords: Community Development, Women Collectives, Women Self Help Group, Women Participation, Women Empowerment, Nutrition, Gender

Introduction

Women Collectives such as Self-help groups (SHGs) are voluntary groups involving 10 to 20 women from similar socio-economic background to attain certain goals. Locally these collectives are called as *samooh, sangh,* or by any local name that means a group. The prime objective of any SHG is to improve the standard of living in terms of development through multiple spheres such as economic, social, political etc. The key engagement of a SHG is to provide economic benefit to the women members of the group in form of providing loans to them. The need for financial assistance was recognised due to low level of literacy and also the non-ownership of assets among women, due to the traditional system where family assets are owned and controlled by male family members (Benni, N., &Barkataky, R., 2018). This pushes women in the area of being marginalised and vulnerable.

The concept of SHGs can be traced back to Mohammed Yunus with the Grameen Bank of Bangladesh. While in India the SHGs were initiated by NABARD around the years 1986-87.This has been recognized as a useful tool in which women of the group come together to save small amount of money regularly which can be later used by members to meet their needs. This micro credit system provides an alternative mechanism to attain economic gains, however women's participation in such collectives have benefits that go beyond the economic aspect. SHGs thrive on group approach, mutual trust and capacity building, on the onus of including each one in this development process. According to ILO (2014), fostering such groups in rural areas becomes important as women in these areas are more isolated and less conscious about their potential in various aspects (Benni, N. &Barkataky, R., 2018).

In India, over the years the shift can be traced from direct individual change to group-oriented approach. There have been various schemes that have existed in past that have landed to the present scheme,Aajeevika - National Rural Livelihoods Mission (NRLM) which was launched by the Ministry of Rural Development (MoRD) in 2011. NRLM aims to enable rural poor by increasing household income through livelihood enhancement and financial services.

There are various forms through which communities engage with each other, such as a group, club. Whereas, collectives have the threshold to engage community people to take collective action towards development through collective approach with participatory learning and action (Gram, L., et al., 2020).

Why are SHGs important?

The SHGs function as a collective unit. While microcredit becomes the primary function for which group members meet every month to collectively save money which is further taken up as loan by a member of the group when in need. The rate of interest is collectively decided by the group members and a leader of each SHG is elected with mutual consent.

Especially in a country like India, where there are various factors that may act as a basis of division. Be it in terms of caste, class, religion, or any other factor for that matter. In such conditions having collectives that bring people together to work towards collective development becomes an important asset. In the case of women, due to traditional practices they don't have ownership over assets or rather are deprive of making decisions on their own. While SHGs in such cases provide them financial benefit along with empowering them.

Figure: Importance of SHGs

Women empowerment through SHG

According to UN, there are five components of women empowerment:

i. Sense of self-worth
ii. Right to determine choices
iii. Right to have access to opportunities and resources
iv. Right to have control over their lives, both within and outside the house
v. Ability to influence direction of social change to create a more just social and economic order, nationally and internationally

The above trajectory of components gets affected by self-help groups. Women's participation in SHGs has gains that are more subtle and gradual. Participation is not used limited to women's presence in the groups. Instead coming together and interactions within the group enables them to open horizons to understand things through another perspective. One such aspect is the gendered dynamics that is present in both, family and community levels. Moreover, learning from engagement in one initiative gets permeated into all aspects of women's lives and helps to break the vicious cycle of gender inequality that affects various facets of their life.

Here, empowerment of women can be understood in terms of their control over their earned finances, awareness about their rights, agency in decision making, make their voice heard. Some instances of such can be understood with visible examples like, woman having equal say in family planning related decisions, having awareness about rights over her own body to make informed choices related to pregnancy, or getting equal share of food as compared to the male members in the family. With their voices heard, women tend to have sense of freedom, improved self-esteem and identity. Such changes have long lasting impacts and just like it is widely said, empowering a woman is equal to empowering a generation. The impact gets permeated to all aspects of woman's life and gets carry forward to the next generation as well.

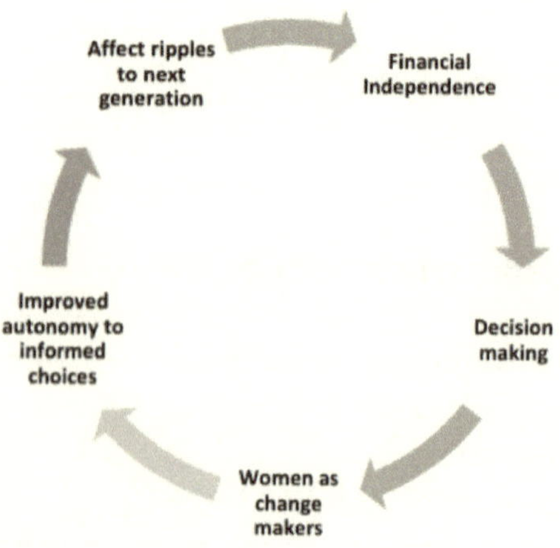

Figure 2: Cycle of empowerment

When women earn themselves, they tend to attain a higher status in the community, with their voices being heard. Several studies have reported that when a woman is earning, her opinions are taken into consideration in matters of decision making. This economic independence gives them self-dependence and motivates to engage in economic and social policies which directly affect them.

Active involvement of women leads them to realize their potential as change makers who can lead families and communities towards positive development. Not just financial independence, but the improved autonomy of women to make informed decisions affects the future generation as well, through gradual shift in improving the conditions of both the self and family.

Women's representation

Under representation of women in communities in terms of their role is something that is widely seen. This can be understood by Caroline Moser's framework that highlights in detail the triple role that women play, with respect to their role in production, reproduction and community affairs, along with the variety of other roles women execute simultaneously that acts as a triple burden for them. In contrast to this, men are more engaged in production related work and those related to community affairs.

The patriarchal structure of the society tends women to be seen in a subordinate position and the tasks in which women are involved, especially household and childcare related are assumed to be their responsibility. As stated by Moser, this gives rise to the practical and strategic gender needs of women. Fulfilling the former will assist women in their current activities. While on the other hand the later, strategic gender needs when met would enable women to transform existing inequity between men and women. These needs refer to the gender dynamics that exists in terms of agency of women in various facets such as decision making, division of labor, voicing their opinions, choices towards positions of power, women's autonomy over their own body to name a few (March, C., 1999).

The strategic gender needs challenge the subordinate position of women in society, making forward to give women 'choice'. For this, engagement of all community members, especially men become important. Making men partners to bring forward issues related to women and adolescents act as a nudge for them to reflect upon their existing status in communities and take steps towards positive social action.

Women participation in development

Enhancing female participation hinges on efforts at addressing cultural stereotypes that project women at the position of subordination. Women who are empowered to take action, often have a positive influence on the lives of other women as well.

The cruciality of women's participation can be easily understood and highlighted by looking at its intergenerational nature. Unequal access makes them susceptible to malnutrition. A nutritional deficient woman is more likely to give birth to a malnourished child. While if the offspring is a girl, then the chances of carry forward of this nutritional malnourishment gets much higher. It's like a vicious cycle. This cycle of vulnerability passes along to the next generation, leading to fewer opportunities for girls to recover from this vicious cycle
(1000 Days, 2020). This malnourished girl child will grow up to be an adolescent and later bear a child of her own. While without access to a healthy diet this cycle will keep on continuing on loop.

Nutrition for women empowerment

Ensuring nutrition of women is a crucial aspect for empowerment. According to
NFHS-4, 53.2% of non-pregnant women and 50.4% of pregnant women are found to be anemic in India. According to Global Burden of Diseases (2019), malnutrition kills more women than any other risk factor that includes tobacco, alcohol, and air pollution. There are various cultural, societal barriers that contribute to act as hurdles for girls and women from accessing healthy, nutritious food. Adequate nutrition is required for proper growth and healthy life. While in girls and women this becomes much more important due to their higher nutritional requirements during adolescence, pregnancy and lactation period. Well-nourished women and girls are likely to be more productive, finish school, become economically independent and further have healthier children (1000 Days, 2020).

Factors such as,

- Women's lack of control in decision making
- Workload, as they tend to work for longer hours
- Household practices like women eating least and last
- Son preference which leads to frequent and poorly spaced pregnancies
- Social norms and myths preventing women and girls from consuming nutrient rich food

Such factors push women and girls into vulnerable positions making them susceptible to malnutrition and micronutrient deficiencies, as these limit the resources available to be spent on availing nutritious rich food.Nutrition and empowerment are interdependent and mutually reinforcing. Having nutrition interventions that are critical and cost effective, enable to have long lasting improvements in the nutritional status of women and girls (1000 Days, 2020).Better nutrition ensures better survival rate that leads to better productivity in terms of education, opportunities, employment, ability to make aware choices and building capacities.

Aspects of nutrition are so important that the Aajeevika- NRLM's *dashasutra* strategy takes this issue into account. The *dashasutra* or ten step strategy focuses on providing holistic upliftment, in which the five areas focus on financial inclusion and financial empowerment, while the other five focus of food, nutrition, health and WASH (FNHW). Here, the SHGs act as platform to leverage to improve the nutritional status of girls and women by initiating targeted nutrition related interventions in communities to ensure long lasting improvements in the nutritional status of women and girls. This allows to look at issues from gendered perspective, identify the existing gender dynamics and take appropriate collective action.

Swabhimaan: A Case study of working through women self-help groups/collectives for promoting nutrition

Interventions such as *Swabhimaan*, dwell on similar lines. 'Swabhimaan' an expression in Hindi language, is used to convey the spirit of self-assertiveness, dignity and self -esteem. Swabhimaan is an initiative, where in various government department services related to health and nutrition are accessed, first by generating awareness about existence of such programmes and schemes among women and also by providing information to them through trained community level resource person, chosen from among the group members only, about the need to optimally use these to support women and adolescent girls nutrition and health needs. It is being implemented inthree eastern Indian states, namely Bihar, Chhattisgarh and Odisha.

It is based on the strength of women Self Help groups mobilised through launched by Government of India's flagship poverty alleviation programme.*Swabhimaan*works in five of the poorest of DAY-NRLM resource blocks, spanning a coverage of 356 villages and reaching out to 5002 SHGs. This programme supports the delivery of a package of 18 essential nutrition interventions via Aajeevika (National Rural Livelihood Mission) promoted village organisations to improve girls 'and women's nutrition before conception, during pregnancy and after birth. It delivers essential nutrition interventions through combination of community actions and systems strengthening led women collectives. The assumption of this programme is that actions will further improve services and practices, thus improving the nutritional status of girls and women.

The primary beneficiaries of this programme are adolescent girls, newlywed couples, pregnant women, mothers of children under two years and secondary target groups are family members and duty bearers at community, block, district level. The intervention's evaluation design is a prospective, non-randomised controlled evaluation for improving food and nutrient intake, preventing micronutrient deficiencies, anaemia, increasing access to health services, water, sanitation and hygiene, education and access and promoting secondary education to delay age at marriage, delaying age at first pregnancy, preventing violence and addressing gender-related issues where women are leading the process.

Women led Intervention

Swabhimaan programme is a synergy between government supported and community led interventions that are systems strengthening actions and the community led actions, respectively. The *Swabhimaan* programme follow the three-tier structure of self-help group (SHG), Village organisation (VO) and Cluster level federation (CLF). The SHG comprises of 8 to 10 women members in each group. This further grows forward to a VO, where
one VO comprises 8 to 10 SHGs. Finally, the top most in this three-tier structure is the CLF that comprises 15 to 20 VOs each. Each tier of the hierarchy has separate functions and roles.

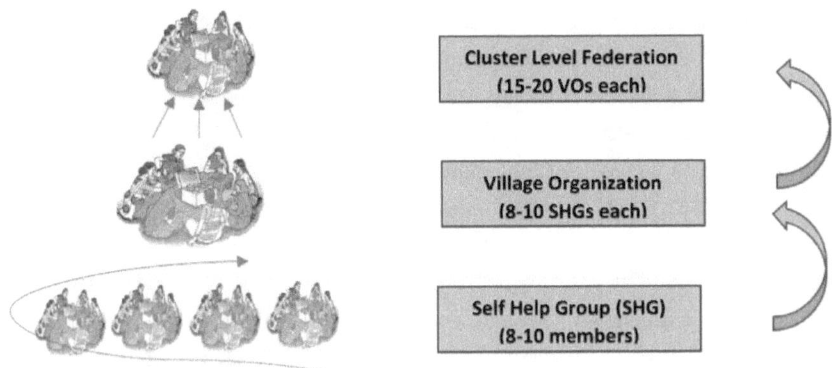

Figure: Three tier system in *Swabhimaan* (Source: ROSHNI-CWCSA)

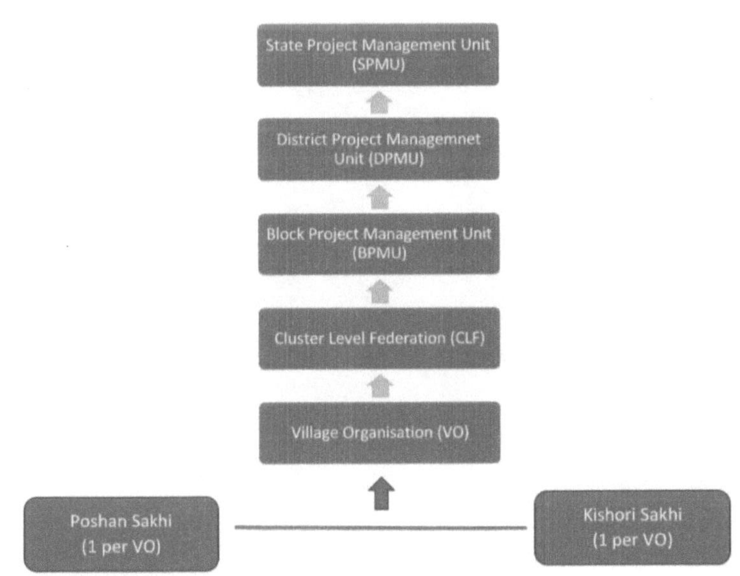

Figure: Implementation of *Swabhimaan* programme

The bottom-upprocess begins with selection of an active woman from the SHG. This active member or Community Resource Person (CRP) undergoes training to work as PoshanSakhi (meaning nutrition friend). In Bihar there is an additional Kishori Sakhi (meaning adolescents' friend) along with Poshan Sakhi who works with the adolescent girls.

Poshan Sakhis, Krishi Mitras (meaning farmer's friend) or VRP (Village Resource Person) are members of VOs who deliver the community led interventions.

The Poshan Sakhis undergo three days pre service training on integrated nutrition microplanning which includes theoretical understanding and practical consultation to identification and prioritization of nutrition and related issues among the target groups (Sethi, 2019). Along with this the Poshan Sakhis undergo training to prepare an annual action plan with a budget to address these problems, identify 'at nutritional risk'adolescent girls and women by anthropometric measures such as MUAC (Mid Upper Arm Circumference) measurements.

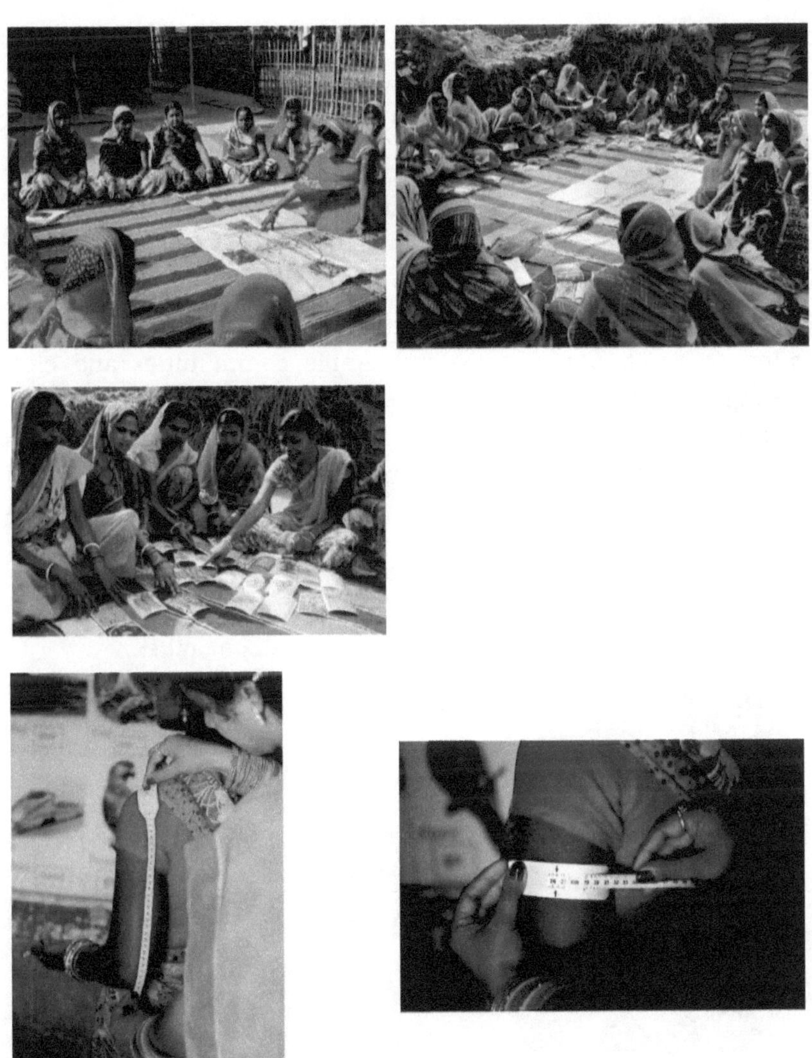

Figure: Glimpse of *Swabhimaan*activities (Source: ROSHNI-CWCSA)

Post training, the PoshanSakhis along with Block Coordinator or Supervisor cofacilitate the development of integrated nutrition microplan(IMP) which is a 12 days process, spread over duration of 2 months in which PoshanSakhis identify the issues present in community under the broader umbrella of FNHW. This IMP process involves microplanning through PLA (Participatory Learning and Action) with a focussed strategy to work on,

- **What** is/are the problems?
- **Why** is it a problem?
- **What can be done**?
- How much **budget** will be required?

FNHW issues related to the community and vulnerable groups are identified, then prioritized according to their severity at the VO level keeping in mind to reach out to most vulnerable communities and clusters. Accordingly, the activities are planned that will be done with the women and adolescent girls groups. After this, the IMPs from all VOs are consolidated at the CLF and block level. The VO monitors the progress and roll out of the microplan developed.

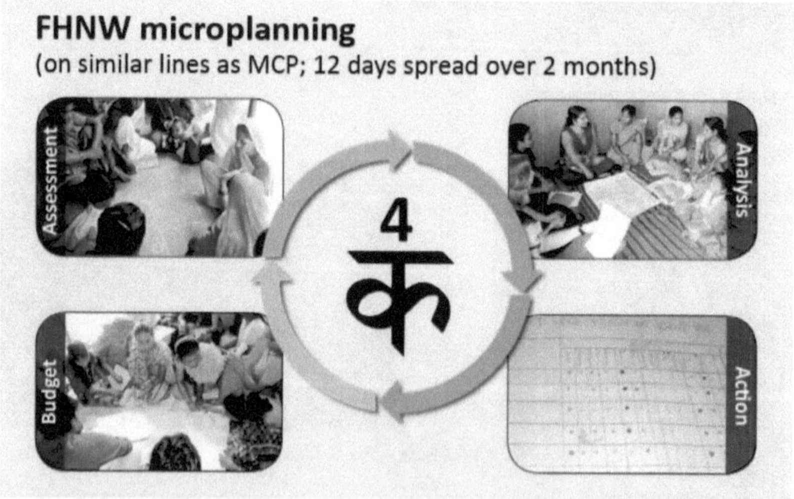

Figure: Integrated Nutrition Microplanning (Source: ROSHNI-CWCSA)

PoshanSakhis are then also trained to conduct PLA meetings with adolescent girls and women groups about the topics, related activities that were identified and strategized in the microplan. The PoshanSakhis receive incentives based on the activities they conduct. While the progress is further reviewed at the CLF level, based on performance indicators (Sethi, 2019).

As mentioned previously, *Swabhimaan*is a package of community led interventions and system strengthening activities. The systems strengthening actions include five components:

- Strengthening ofVHSNDs to improve access to family planning, antenatal care, micronutrient supplements, monthly review of nutrition indicators, identification of at risk of undernutrition i.e., women with MUAC <23 cm and adolescent girls with MUAC <19 cm.
- Strengthening adolescent health days to improve access to health and nutrition services
- Extended VHSND once in every 6 months for newlywed and women, which includes individual counselling and information about entitlement camps
- Annual trainings and follow up meetings with service providers from ICDS, water and sanitation departments, food security to improve delivery of entitlements and services
- Ensuring regular review meetings with representation across government departments involved in service delivery

Here, in addition to DAY-NRLM, the line departments such as Department of Women and Child Department, Department of Health and Family Welfare, Department of Water and Sanitation, Department of Civil and Food Supply are involved in system strengthen activities to improve ICDS reach, strengthen VHSND, improving water quality, increasing coverage of food subsidy schemes, respectively.

The PoshanSakhi along with frontline workers, ASHA, ANM and AWW ensure that these activities reach out to the vulnerable groups and beneficiaries. PoshanSakhis are present in the villages, so they enable the process of mobilising women to avail services from the VHSND, Anganwadi centres. Activities such as vaccination, availing micronutrient (Calcium, IFA) supplements, home visits to at nutrition risk women and adolescent girls, antenatal services, linking beneficiaries to VHSND in order to avail anthropometric check-ups, enrolling drop out girls back to school, developing nutri garden in households, counselling on family planning methods etc. All these activities take place in convergence of the PoshanSakhi, ASHA, AWW and ANM.

Role of each tier of women collectives in community development activities

Cluster Level Federation (CLF)

The CLF undertakes the responsibility of stock taking of FNHW microplan, newlywed couple meetings, training of Community Resource person (CRP) / PoshanSakhi and VRP, participate in block convergent review meetings, linking families of at nutrition risk women and adolescent girls to social protection and agri-poultry schemes, entitlement camps and health check-ups for SHG members. Along with these, providing loans for secondary education and making farmer field school sites.

Village Organisation (VO)

VO undertakes the role of selection of PoshanSakhi and developingnutritionmicroplan. Conducting awareness drives on social issues,maitrikisaanbaithak (meaning friendly farmer meeting) on nutrition sensitive agriculture,maitribaithak by using PLA activities. The PoshanSakhi identifies at nutrition risk women during the VO meetings.

Self Help Groups (SHG)

Under the existing DAY-NRLM structure there are four SHG meetings that happen in a month. Out of these, one meeting is focussed on conducting FNHW activities planned through the microplan strategy. In this one meeting the planned activities are conducted with use of PLAs.

PoshanSakhis support frontline workers (ANM, ASHA, AWW) in providing counselling and key messages on diet diversity, elicit information about importance of maternal health. They also do fortnightly visits to at nutrition risk women to monitor, counsel them for regular health check ups and encourage them to develop nutri gardens in their household. They also conduct food demonstration and counselling sessions to encourage diet diversity, consumption of locally available nutritious foods. Similarly, the KishoriSakhi (present in Bihar *Swabhimaan*site) works with adolescent girls in the area to promote diet diversity, encourage completion of education, awareness about hygiene practices etc.

Also, PoshanSakhis conduct monthly Parivaar Chaupal baithak (meaning family meeting) to engage family members especially men and mother in laws to ensure improvement of nutritional status of women and girls. The concept of Parivaar Chaupal stems from the societal norms that decisions related to food intake, availing services, family planning, dietary practices are primarily influenced by the decision makers in the family, who are mostly husbands and mother in laws. The 12 meetings in ParivaarChaupal are designed to be held at a common platform with family members and influential members of community using PLA to address existing norms and practices that deteriorate the nutritional status of women and girls and puts them at a vulnerable position. Such platform helps in perceiving the gender dynamics to address issues such as domestic violence, early pregnancy, family planning, myths related to food intake, interspousal communication, division of labour, eating practices at households as these directly impact the nutrition and health of women.

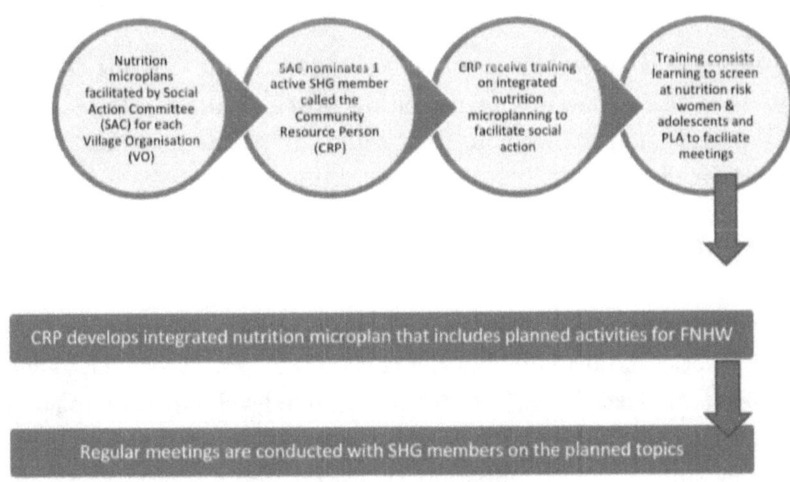

Figure 1: Process of *Swabhimaan*initiative

Along with these activities, *Swabhimaan*also comprises of Nutrition Sensitive Integrated Farming Systems (NSIFS) that links agriculture and nutrition to bring forward nutrition sensitive approach. The Krishi Mitra or VRP works and sensitises women farmers to adopt practices that improve nutrition availability at household level. This involves integration of various ecosystems like poultry, fishery, cattle to secure food diversity. Nutri sensitive is a pathway to ensure improved nutrient efficiency of the available food items. Some of such approaches are in the form of developing nutri garden at home to avail low-cost nutritious produce, adopting sack farming that enables landless farmers or those who have marginal landholding.

The focus of the programme is that systems actions and community actions will together nudge services and practices to eventually improve the nutritional status of women and adolescent girls. The members of Self-help groups are able to avail their entitled services, engage in nutrition-based livelihoods, participate in activities for behavior change. Nutrition focused interventions leveraged though women groups have potential to improve the nutritional status of women and girls, if engaged with whole communities (Desai, et al., 2020).

Awareness and Knowledge

SHGs as a platform enables to collectively identify the existing community norms that act as barriers in providing proper nutrition to women and girls. Women get to know about their rights, entitlements and access to the available services

Promote behavior change

Through meetings, the PoshanSakhi disseminates knowledge about healthy dietary practices and highlights the community practices such as women eating least and last, that affects her nutritional level. Encouraging to adopt practices like backyard poultry, nutrition garden improves the chances of women getting access to nutrition rich food items, along with behavior change related toappropriate sanitation practices

Access to services

As a collective, women get aware of their services they are entitled to so that they can avail them. Such as benefits of supplementation received from Anganwadi centres in the form of iron, calcium tablets, antenatal, immunization services, anthropometricmeasurements to calculate the status of nutrition and exposure to other services that women and girls are entitled to

Building Capacities

As part of collectives, women build capacities that provides them perspective to take up decisions and make informed choices

Integrated approach

Develops autonomy and capacities of women to have a voice to become equal partners in decision making in households related to matters of family planning, nutritional choices, etc.

Women groups collectively lead a way to improve the nutritional status of women and girls by enabling them to become equal partners in household.When it comes to improving nutritional status of women, then having them address the issue and come up with a solution becomes a community driven approach.

Challenges

Most of the success stories about women are about the struggles they have to come across in order to achieve their goals. If seen from other perspective this also indicates the inequity that women have to face in the society.

- Education: Lower literacy rates among women may act as a hurdle for them while eliciting further information
- Work family balance: Creating a balance between the responsibilities at household and those of the collective may become a task for women
- Mobilizing men: Due to the patriarchal structure, engaging men for social action can act as a challenge for women
- Existing norms in society: Present norms and practices of the community might come in way of implementing the desired social practice
- Monetary gain: In many cases, women are urged by their families to join SHGs in anticipation of immediate monetary returns and when that doesn't happen, they might be pressured to withdraw themselves from the group

Conclusions

Involving women for community development is crucial in order to ensure sustainable growth and betterment of the community at large. Increasing women's participation in community activities not just provides them opportunities to voice their thoughts, but at the same time this acts as a roadway to address together the existing cultural norms & stereotypes in the communityleading to a holistic development and betterment of the community at large which will be sustainable for years to follow. Women collectives serve as a platform to address the existing causes of malnourishment and undernutrition in women. Having them engage and collectively work towards improvement of nutrition status offers to bring about a potential solution, while empowering women in this process enabling more livelihood options, providing women bargaining power within households to make informed decisions.

References

1. Benni, N., &Barkataky, R. (2018). *The role of the Self-Employed Women's Association (SEWA) in providing financial services to rural women*: FAO & SEWA

2. Brody, C., Hoop, T., Vojtkova, M., et al. (2015). Economic Self-Help group Programs for Improving Women's Empowerment: A Systematic Review. *Campbell Systematic Reviews*, *11*(1), 1–182. https://doi.org/10.4073/csr.2015.19

3. DAY-NRLM. (2017). *A Handbook on SHG - Bank Linkage*

4. Desai, S., Misra, M., Das, A., et al. (2020). Community interventions with women's groups to improve women's and children's health in India: a mixed-methods systematic review of effects, enablers and barriers. *BMJ Global Health*, *5*(12), e003304. https://doi.org/10.1136/bmjgh-2020-003304

5. Fonchingong, C. C. (2006). Expanding horizons: Women's voices in community-driven development in the Cameroon grasslands. *GeoJournal*, *65*(3), 137–149. https://doi.org/10.1007/s10708-005-3597-y

6. FAO (2013). The State of Food and Agriculture.

7. *Global Burden of Disease (GBD 2019)*. (2020, December 9). Institute for Health Metrics and Evaluation. http://www.healthdata.org/gbd/2019

8. Gram, L., Desai, S., & Prost, A. (2020). Classroom, club or collective? Three types of community-based group intervention and why they matter for health. *BMJ Global Health, 5*(12), e003302. https://doi.org/10.1136/bmjgh-2020-003302

9. International Food Policy Research Institute. (2019). *Engaging women's groups to improve nutrition.* http://ebrary.ifpri.org/utils/getfile/collection/p15738coll5/id/6808/filename/6810.pdf

10. March, C., Smyth, I., & Mukhopadhyay, M. (1999). *A guide to gender-Analysis Framework.* Oxfam.

11. Roshni- Centre of Women Collectives Led Social Action. http://roshni-cwcsa.co.in/ Accessed on 8th May 2021.

12. Sethi, V., Bhanot, A., Bhattacharjee, S., et al. (2019). Integrated multisectoral strategy to improve girls' and women's nutrition before conception, during pregnancy and after birth in India (Swabhimaan): protocol for a prospective, non-randomised controlled evaluation. *BMJ Open, 9*(11), e031632. https://doi.org/10.1136/bmjopen-2019-031632

13. Sethi, V., Bhanot, A., Bhalla, S., et al. (2017). Partnering with women collectives for delivering essential women's nutrition interventions in tribal areas of eastern India: a scoping study. *Journal of Health, Population and Nutrition, 36*(1). https://doi.org/10.1186/s41043-017-0099-8

14. The Lancet. (2015). Women are the key to sustainable development. *The Lancet, 386*(9999), 1110. https://doi.org/10.1016/s0140-6736(15)00248-2

15. Tshuma, D., &Kajala, E. (2016, November 23). *Empower Women - Five major components of women's empowerment.* EmpowerWomen. https://www.empowerwomen.org/en/community/discussions/2016/11/five-major-components-of-womens-empowerment

16. 1000Days. (2020). *Nourishing Gender Equality: How Nutrition Interventions are an Underleveraged Tool in the Fight for Women's Rights:* Author.

VIII

Women Entrepreneur: Rocks

Dr.Deepa Swamy
Associate Professor
Govt Arts Girls College, Kota
Email Id: deepaswamy9@gmail.com

Abstract

The role of women is a fundamental question for the development of all societies. Development means that development is political, social, economic, cultural & other dimensions of human life as well as the development of economic and other material resources. Based on the general concept of an entrepreneur, women entrepreneur is one who owes as well as operates the enterprise i.e.

i Enterprise which are exclusively operates by women.

ii. Enterprise where 51% of capital is owns by women.

iii. 50 % of total labour employed are women functions of women entrepreneur.

This has been welcomed and efforts made to incorporate not only in political and social structure but also in the economic sphere. Women are equally involved with motivation and managerial capabilities, in starting and running small enterprise. According to development of women entrepreneur five major types of women entrepreneurs are their i.e. affluent entrepreneur, push factor, pull factor, rural entrepreneur, self-employed entrepreneur.

There are different qualities of women entrepreneur like hard work, patience, managerial qualities, risk taking capacity etc. More than professional educator women entrepreneur should be innovator as well as risk taker. She should have quality to face male competition of society to give heights to her enterprise. Indian women entrepreneur are changing by moving in non-traditional sector from traditional sector. Even in some areas women are giving better results than male counter parts. There are different problems faced by Indian women entrepreneurs to run and enrich their enterprise like lack of experience, funding problem, problem of mobility etc. In spite of different problems women entrepreneur are finding spectrum in traditional as well as non-traditional industries and these positive attitude will definitely provide economic growth to industry.

Keywords : Women Entrepreneurs, Enterprise, Entrepreneurship .

Introduction

"No society could progress unless women who constitute half of its population are given equal opportunities" said by Late Prime Minister of India Smt. Indira Gandhi.

The role of women is a fundamental question for the development of all societies. Development means total development in political, social, economic, cultural & other dimensions of human life as well as the development of economic and other material resources.

Today, it is held 2/3 of all the work in the world is performed by women yet the women are rated as "non-worker" having the least management role to play in the socio economic system. This is just because in traditional societies women were confined to four walls of home, children and family. But emancipation of women is one of the genotype of economic development and social progress.

Entrepreneurship among women is a recent phenomenon in developing country like India; they represent a group who have forged a new identity for them. Women entrepreneur are group of women who have broken away the beaten tracks and are exploring new vistas of economic participation. The present century having taken greater strides of prosperity has helped women entrepreneur from within the four walls into a vast shield of opportunities uncovering their potential and installing in them the fruits of independence.

It takes a great deal of courage and desire of her to actually try to become an entrepreneur and she also need persistence and determination to succeed in the effort. It is, therefore, very important for the facilitation to assist the women to gain courage, persistence and along desire to become an entrepreneur as well as the confidence that she can do so.

Based on the general concept of an entrepreneur, women entrepreneur is one who owes as well as operates/runs the enterprise i.e.

i. Enterprise which are exclusively operates by women.

ii. Enterprise where 51% of capital is owns by women.

iii. 50 % of total labour employed are women.

Qualities of women entrepreneur

a) Good Administrator

Women is the whole soul of enterprise run by her. So, to lead success of enterprise has to plan execute, monitor and also take feedback administrate about all activities run in the organisation. Women should be good administrator to lead success for an enterprise.

b) Innovation

For grand success of any enterprise innovation plays an important role. So, to enhance the activity new and risky women entrepreneur has to put ideas in their enterprise. Ideas that provides new heights and different benefits to enterprise.

c) Risk Taking

Entrepreneur is an risk taking activity more risk more benefits. Arising the risk in economic and non – economic activities can give growth to the enterprise.

d) Exploring Oneself

If women entrepreneur has to explore a business unit she has to perform business opportunity survey. Market survey help to launch as well as explore business.Exploring should not be limited to market but also for consumer, new technology, new programme and policies etc.

e) Leadership

Without leadership in any industry success can't be taken.Right guidance at right timecan make success story for enterprise. So, quality of leadership is one of the most important for women entrepreneur.

f) Motivator

For providing heights to the industry, women entrepreneur should play the role of motivator. This quality will definitely boost the energy level of worker. If worker is in high energy than no one can stop industry in getting heights.

g) Accept Challenge

New challenges always comes in a way of developing or even to developed enterprise. No doubt these challenges will increase for women entrepreneur as compare to man due to different conditions

h) Hard Work

For Performing dual duty as an home maker as well as entrepreneur is not easy. To complete dual duty lady has to perform hard work both physically as well as mentally with patience. And as we all know that hard work always pay success.

i) Patience

Patience is another phenomenon to be successful entrepreneur. No doubt women have more patience that man. That is why she can perform not only householder task as well as enterprise task. When we talk about enterprise some time risk taking factors or innovative ideas need time to bloom where patience is an important factor.

More than to professional educator women entrepreneur should be innovator as well as risk taker. She should have quality to face male competition of society to give heights to her enterprise.Indian women entrepreneur are changing by moving in non-traditional sector from traditional sector. Even in same areas women are giving both results than male counter parts.

Problems of Women Entrepreneur

In Indian context women entrepreneur has to cross words from society more than male counter parts. Same enterprise but more struggle just because of being women. Problems faced by women entrepreneur:

a) Lack of Funds

Lack of awareness among women leads to lack of fund. Govt. Of India is launching different scheme time to time but women's are not aware of these scheme. Compare to large/big entrepreneur small entrepreneur experiences more financial problem. They don't try to enjoy bank credit but suffer from working capital problem. Instead of taking loan from banks they prefer to take loan from middle man and money landers who give loan on high rate of interest. Even after good financial conditions of family preference is for male than female.

b) Less risk bearing capacity

Especially in Indian context, due to extraordinary protection from society and family, risk bearing capacity of women is being decreased. Even due to protection, confidence level is decreases. This is big hurdle in becoming successful entrepreneur.

c) Less Motivation

When we talk about India, moving out of women for jobs are not motivational. They are motivated to become housewives, mother and home makers. If these multiple role are played by women, male dominating society are satisfied but when they break track to become women entrepreneur they are never motivated. Lack of motivation is another great restriction in women path of becoming entrepreneur.

d) Lack of family support

Women has to play dual role of women entrepreneur as well as of home maker. Their family always support them to become house maker instead of women entrepreneur. Due to different challenges in entrepreneur with support of family; becoming women entrepreneur always an secondary preference by women. Even in some cases work exploitation of women is done by family members. We all know that support of family is very necessary for any type development.

e) Lack of Education

Women are always discouraged to get higher education than male family members. Rather than this we can say that illiteracy problem is widespread among women. Due to lack of quality education, it becomes challenges in setting and running enterprise for women.

f) Lack of Equality

Indian society is an male dominating, where male ego always become barrier in success of women entrepreneur. Women has to forget her success in entrepreneurial activities.Gender biasness is biggest empty space in growth of women entrepreneur.

g) Lack of Infrastructure

In male dominating society of India preference is always given to male members. Women has to run their enterprise from residential premises. Dual work of home maker and entrepreneurs can be played comfortably in the residential premises. In residential premises there will always be lack of infrastructures and less chance of growth.

h) Marketing Ability

Generally women entrepreneur are on back foot when it comes to marketing. Even with high quality of products and services in marketing strategy women defect due to different reasons. So, this can be counted as another major lacuna for women entrepreneur.

i) Lack of mobility

For success of enterprise it is necessary to travel from one area to another for business work. Not even from city to another city but within city. Domestic responsibilities restrict the mobility of women. To avoid mobility they appoint middle man which increase the path length of success for women.

j) Lack of experience

Experience can be gain by performing task. There are way long to gain experience in enterprise for women. This lack of information and experience hurdle in handling entrepreneurial activities successfully.

A women entrepreneur has an eye for opportunities, an uncanny vision commercial ability to take risk with an adventure spirit women are more receptive to dies and are open to change, more confident of future without disturbing their pivoted role in the family.(Nair 1980)

Development of women itself been dependent upon the socio cultural atmosphere of the family. Development of women is being visualised in any field of activities is due to strength of women entrepreneur. Women have tried to overcome the biased outlook and approaches of the society in many cases of therefore entered in different walks of life for participate in social, political and economic activities of the country. In spirit of being labelled as weaker segment for household affairs a number of women have entered into the self-employment activities. Time to time different researches shows that women participation in entrepreneurial activities are increasing day by day.

This has been welcomed and efforts made to incorporate not only in political and social structure but also in the economic sphere. Women are equally involved with motivation and managerial capabilities, in starting and running small enterprise.

Types of women enterprise: According to their making

a) Affluent entrepreneurs

These types of entrepreneurs belongs to businessman family. They are financially strong and know the basic trick of business. Necessary resources to start new enterprise can be easily available for them. They are always motivated by their family to join family business or start new enterprise. They rarely suffer from lack of finance.

b) Pull factor

These are risk taking urban educated women. They generally start enterprise with the help of financial institutions. They enjoy financial independency started by themselves. They have good amount of confidence which help to remove all type of barrier.

c) Push factor

When women struggle from financial difficulties they move toward business activities. In push factors this type of women manage their family business or start new business in different adverse family situation. In this case women become entrepreneurs for sake of family finance. Generally they run small or cottage industry.

d) Rural Entrepreneur

As the name indicates these entrepreneur belongs to rural area so there is an low investment with minimum risk and less benefit. They don't move for big opportunities. They also like to run their firm at home.

e) Self Employed Entrepreneur

These type of entrepreneur belongs to below poverty line. They generally choose tiny enterprise with financial support for their family.

The most important things that a woman needs in order to be successful entrepreneur is to become empowered. Managerial role played by women provide victory to the enterprise. Proper decision making increase income as well as production level of industry

It takes a great deal of courage and desire of her to actually try to become an entrepreneur and she also need persistence our determination of succeed in effort. It is, therefore, very important for the facilitation to assist the women to gain courage, persistence and a strong desire to become an entrepreneur as well as the confidence that she can do as.Inspite of different problems women entrepreneur are finding spectrum in traditional as well as non-traditional industries and these positive attitude will definitely provide economic growth to industry.

Entrepreneurship Concept

The ability to develop, run, organise, promote the enterprise to earn profit. Another synonyms of entrepreneurship can be starting a new enterprise/ business. In the term of economic when profit is earn with the connection of land, labour, management, resources with different process it is called entrepreneurship.

In Indian economy entrepreneurship plays a important role. Entrepreneurship develop different type of job. Not only type but at of different level while and grey collar job. Job for skilled, unskilled, literate, illiterate workers. Implementation of different innovation idea can be done only through entrepreneurship. No society could progress until and unless the base of entrepreneurship/enterprise is strong. Any type of community development like making infrastructure higher education or increasing standard of living can be done through developing variety of enterprise in society.

Increasing standard of living is directly propionate to increase of income. Increase of income can be lose through development of different entrepreneurial activities. When we talk about increase in standard of living that consumption of goods and services by household activities. When there is more consumption of goods and services and there that increases that support research and development as there is always demand of new product and services. Promotion in research and production will directly increases the development of economy.

Few recommendation for development of women entrepreneur

- Ability of women entrepreneurs should be increases through training, meetings, research, motivational lecture, especially based on women entrepreneur.
- In working place confirm child care centres should be there.
- Equal opportunities and treatment should be given to women at their worker place.
- It is a duty of society to listen and the react according to the voice of women entrepreneur.
- Not only financial but also different facilities should be provided at the door step of women entrepreneurs for growth and development.
- There is an need of the era that women entrepreneur should not be on paper but also the real life. Strict laws should be implemented by government in this case.
- Network for women entrepreneurs should be promoted & developed. Even this can be done through different platform of social media. Through proper network strength, weakness, opportunities and threats can be easily find of any business run by women.
- Strength and opportunities should be motivated and weakness and threats should be removed after finding reasons.
- Equal wages and responsibilities should be given women for growth.
- Government offices should be created exclusively by the women and for the women which provide facility and take responsibility of women entrepreneur.
- Different bold steps should be taken to provide financial stability for women. Women Entrepreneurs are still not aware of different scheme given by government to women entrepreneurs. So by awareness camp and other methods these scheme should be reached to women entrepreneur at right time.
- Outlook of society towards women entrepreneurs should be changed.

Some resources for funding and support for women entrepreneurs

Growth ratio of women entrepreneurs in India is increased in last few days. To start an enterprise different human as well as non-human resources are required to start enterprise but among these resource. Capital(Money) is the most important

There are some schemes launched by government of India in different interval of time which provide benefits to women entrepreneurs which offers flexible or low ratio of interest on loans. Even some loans are collateral free. Different programmes are launched by government which give motivation, knowledge, about women enterprise. Many scheme are available which are hard to summarised in this chapter but some schemes are:

1. Trades Related Entrepreneurship Assistant and Development (TREAD) scheme:

Ministry of micro, small & medium enterprise offers this scheme to promote women entrepreneurs. Government also grants loan up to 30 lakhs in this scheme. Women are empower here in activities of trading. All information regarding trading, having activities, information, counselling activities can be greater here by women entrepreneur.

2. Rashtriya Mahila Kosh (RMK):

This programme was launched in 1993 by Ministry of women and child Development. Micro credits are provided to women entrepreneurs for informal sector. (Informal sectors are those enterprise which are not register in government). Self Help groups(SHG'S) can get loan through intermediary organisations which directly get loan from RashtriyaMahilaKosh (RMK).

3. Stand Up Scheme:

To promote women entrepreneurs from SC/ST category loans are provide in this scheme. Women can enjoy loan from Rs.10 lakh to Rs. 1crore. Loan are provided for new and recently set up industry. Under this scheme women can take loan for manufacturing, services or trading sector. This scheme was launched on 5th April 2016.

4. Mudra Yojana Scheme for women:

This scheme is launched by government of India for small units of women entrepreneurs. This can be used to set up small units like beauty parlour, dance unit, tailoring unit, day care centre, food unit , tuition centre etc. collateral guarantors below 10 lakh loan is not required. This scheme has three plans which are divided according to loan credit i.e. Shishu (loan up to Rs. 50,000), Kishore (loan from Rs. 50,000 to Rs. 5 lakh) and Tarun (loan from Rs. 5 lakh to Rs. 10 lakh)

5. Dena Shakti:

This is scheme which provide finance to women entrepreneurs for different activities at micro as well as small level. Some of these activities are agriculture sector, small enterprise (service and manufacturing sector) and trade sector.

6. MaanDeshi Foundation:

This scheme is for rural women entrepreneurs who like to expand their to enterprise, create new products, it provides banking service at the door step as well as insurance scheme.

Banks

Different Nationalised banks as well as no nationalised banks provide many new and different schemes to support women entrepreneurs. like:

1. Economic independence scheme for empowering women be ICICI Bank:

Exclusively for underprivileged women of rural India this scheme was developed. It helps women to like to start or expand their enterprise. By promoting entrepreneurship among rural women to earn sectional livelihoods.

2. Bharatiya Mahila Bank:

With the goal to finance underprivileged women entrepreneur this bank was started. It was merged with State Bank Of India in year 2017. Loan up to Rupees 20 crores are offer by this bank.

3. Cent Kalyani scheme:

Under this scheme loan is provide to women who run small and medium enterprise in agriculture as well as retail and trading sector. Loan of Rupees 100 lakh can be sanctioned without any guarantor to women. These loans are offer by each bank of India.

4. Mahila Udhyam Nidhi Scheme:

Punjab National Bank launched this scheme for women who wants to setup their new projects where loan can be sanctioned up to Rupees 10 lakh.

5. Annapurna Scheme:

Women who adopt food catering business can go for this scheme. This scheme is launched by BharatiyaMahila Bank (Now SBI) and State Bank of Mysore. Without any collateral women can enjoy loan up to Rupees 50,000 with repayment period of these years.

Conclusions

Women are now in the lead role to develop country. Women entrepreneurs on the developing world make a large and often unrecognised contribution to their countries economic development. Entrepreneurship itself is recently being recognised as a full-fledged profession and women entrepreneurs is an even newer phenomenon. Thus, we as a society should support this newer phenomenon for all round growth of the country. The need of the day to support, recognised and established women entrepreneurs for economic growth of country.

References

1. Goyal M, Parkash J., (2011) Women entrepreneurship in India-problems and prospects. International Journal of Multidisciplinary Research; Sep 1(5):195-207.
2. Kumbhar, V. (2013) Some Critical Issues of Women Entrepreneurship in Rural India. European Academic Research; 1 (2): 192-200
3. Saurabh S. (2012) Issues and Challenges faced by Women entrepreneurs and their training needs. SHIV SHAKTI International Journal of in Multidisciplinary and Academic Research (SSIJMAR).1(2):1-8.
4. Siddiqui AB. (2012) Problems encountered by women entrepreneurs in India. International Journal of Applied Research & Studies. Sep;1(2):1-2.

IX

Improving the Quality of Life of Farm Families through Integrated Strategic Interventions

Dr. L. Uma Devi[1] and Dr. Bilquis[2]

[1]Professor and Dean of Community Science and [2]Associate Professor and Head (HDFS),

College of Home Science, ANGRAU, Guntur

Email Id: bilquisasha@gmail.com

Abstract

The present study was taken up to evolve a suitable intervention model for improving the quality of life of farm families. Different strategies were integrated in the intervention for better outcomes. An experimental design was adopted for the purpose of study. The sample was 90 which included the infants, mothers and adolescents of farm families. Interview schedule and standardized scales were used to measure the knowledge, psychomotor development, life skills and life satisfaction of the participants. The study concluded that intervention programmes should be planned in an integrated manner instead of isolated method for better outcomes. Health, nutrition, development and life skills are all important factors that contribute for the overall life satisfaction. Family approach while giving intervention is proven to be the best method where the needs of all the family members are addressed and enhanced through integrated approach.

Introduction

Rural families lack access to quality health and nutrition services required to improve their quality of life. Addressing the health and nutritional needs of farm families is the need of the day. Farm families lack knowledge and skills to enrich their because of illiteracy and ignorance lives. The Government is providing these services through various programmes like ICDS and schemes which proved to be not effective in meeting the end needs due to lapses in implementation and lack of successful model to provide these services in an integrated manner.

Nutrition and health interventions are being taken up in several government programmes including the Integrated Child Development Services (ICDS) programme, the Public Distribution System (PDS), the Midday Meal Scheme (MMS), the Total Sanitation Campaign (TSC) and National Rural Health Mission (NRHM). However, India lacks a comprehensive, national health and nutrition strategy and linkages between planning, managing, and implementing these interventions. Majority of the programs are plagued with severe operational problems, particularly in governance.

Nutrition need to be effectively integrated into a larger health strategy. Though few efforts to integrate nutrition into NRHM and ICDS were done these interventions could not address the problems of infant and maternal mortality (Gupta & Khaira, 2008; Shrinivasan & Shekhar, 2007).

Improving the health and nutrition status of farm families is the need of the day. This project aims at providing the health and nutrition interventions coupled with life skill enhancement to cope up with the adverse situations in agriculture as well as in life. Farmer can focus on agriculture and put his heart and soul in agriculture only when his family is healthy and happy. For this the family needs to be equipped with sufficient knowledge about nutrition, health and life skills aspects which would enable them to access various resources eventually.

Focusing on these lines an integrated strategic intervention model would be evolved in this project wherein the knowledge and skill interventions would be taken up to bring the desirable change in the lives of farm families.

This project would be a pilot study to establish the evidence on an integrated approach and strategic interventions which improve the nutritional and health status thereby improving the quality of life of farming community.

General Objective

Improving the quality of life of farm families through integrated strategic interventions

Specific Objectives

- To study the Nutritional and health needs of farm women and children
- To provide nutrition and family health care intervention to farm women and children
- To provide life skills education to farm families
- To assess the impact of intervention on improving the knowledge and skills of farm families
- To study the level of life satisfaction of the farm families after giving integrated strategic interventions.
- Evolving a suitable intervention model for improving the quality of life of farm families

Methods and Materials

Research design

Research design is a systematic investigation of study materials and sources in order to establish facts and research new conclusions. A research design encompasses the methodology and procedures employed to conduct scientific research.

Experimental research design

Pre –Post experimental research design was chosen for the purpose of study.

Sampling procedure

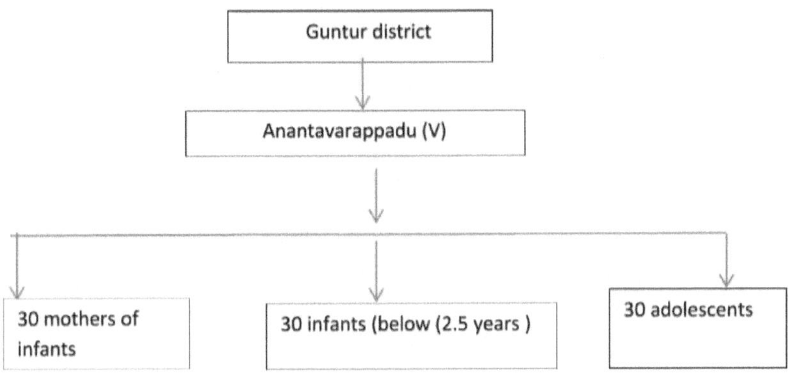

Location of the study

The present study was taken up in the Ananthavarappadu village of Guntur district.

Sampling technique

Purposive Random sampling method was used for the selecting sample. The farm families having infants below 2.5 years of age were selected purposively for carrying out the intervention study. Infants and Adolescents were selected with the help of local Anganwadi teacher. Farm families were identified with the help of SHG leaders.

Tools Used for the study

S.NO		
1	Interview Schedules (Uma Devi, Bilquis & Sudharani	To assess the health and nutritional knowledge of rural mothers.
2	Developmental Assessment Scales for Indian Infants (Pramila Pathak, 1997)	To assess the Psychomotor development of the infants
3	Life skills Scale (Anuradha, 2005)	To assess the life skills levels
4	Life Satisfaction Scale (Promila Singh and George Joseph 1996)	To assess the satisfaction of life levels.

Data Collection

The investigators personally visited the rural area and obtained permission from Anganwadi centre of the area and the sample was identified using purposive random sampling technique. The data was collected on general information, nutritional and health practices, infant stimulation and life skills of the adolescents by using selected families.

Data collection from Infants

Infant mothers were interviewed about various scientific child rearing practices and stimulatory practices adopted for optimum development. Later experimental group mothers were given intervention about importance of stimulation for infants growth and development. Developmental status of infants was assessed by using a checklist of milestones .The total score obtained in each developmental domain was calculated based on the activities performed by the infants. Physical, Psycho-motor, language and socio-emotional aspects. Based on the scores infants were categorised as good/ average and poor.

Data collection from Adolescents

Data from adolescents was collected by using the life skills questionnaire. Adolescents were interviewed individually by making home visits. The total life skill score and sub dimension wise scores were calculated and categorized as good/ average and poor

Data collection from farm women

Data from farm women was collected by making home visits. Interview schedule in local language was developed to study the knowledge of farm women in the areas of health, nutrition and life satisfaction. The questions given in the schedule were given options Yes/ No .the correct answer was given one mark and wrong was scored as zero. The total score of the schedule was categorized as Good/ Average/Poor levels of knowledge.

Methods of data collection

individual home visits, focused group discussions, personal interviews.

Intervention programmes

Intervention packages on health and nutrition, psychomotor development of children were used for the purpose of the study .Standardized intervention packages are used for the study developed by AICRP –CD, PJTSAU. Intervention was given to the individual mothers, infants, adolescents using the standardized intervention packages. A detailed intervention package which included the following components was developed to be used with the infants, adolescents, and farm women.

Intervention strategies

Various strategies used for educating the farm women and adolescents were

-

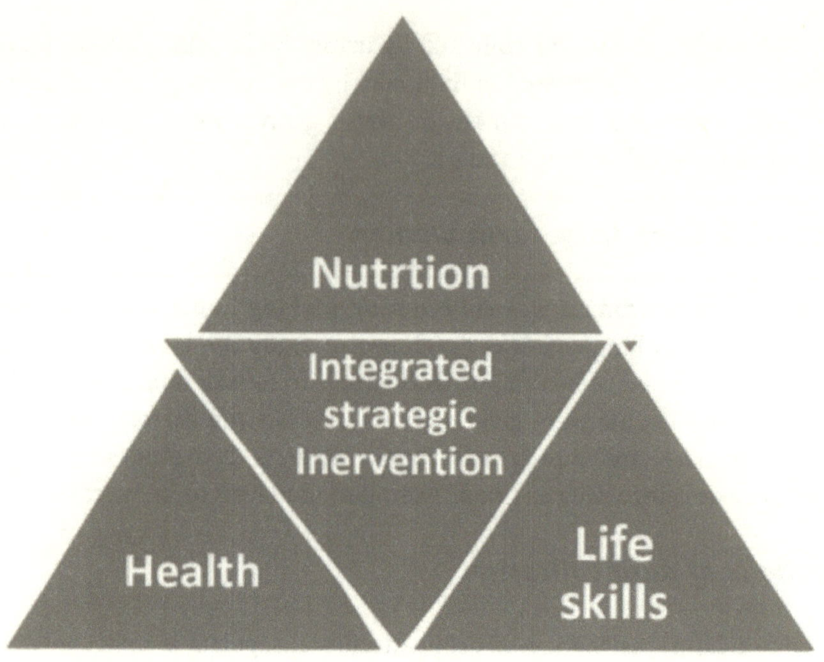

Nutrition intervention strategies

- Nutrition education
- Promoting nutritional garden
- Enriching the diets with low cost nutritious foods

Health care intervention strategies

- Reproductive & child health education
- Demonstrations & group discussions on scientific child rearing practices, Infant stimulation, Immunization.
- Focused group interviews

Life skills education strategies

- Stress management through group counseling, yoga
- Crisis management
- Communication skills & decision making skills through one to one contacts and small group discussions

Pre-test

Initial assessment of the knowledge levels of the rural mothers, infants and adolescents was done using the pre-test schedule. Infant assessed for their mental and psychomotor development using DASII scale. A life satisfaction scale was used to assess the quality of life of rural women.

Implementation of intervention programme

Based on the knowledge of the mothers of infants and adolescents in the areas of health, nutrition, life skills components during pre –test, intervention programmes was planned to increase their knowledge levels and improve the developmental status of infants. The intervention programme was implemented for period of 6 months.

Intervention was planned separately to the infant mothers, farm women and Adolescents. Mothers of infant babies were given education about the scientific child care practices, importance of stimulation, areas of stimulation and indigenous play material that can be used for giving stimulation were explained.

Similarly adolescents were given education about various life skills like decision-making, critical thinking, conflict management, problem solving skills by using a standardized educational package in local language.

Farm women were given educational intervention on the health care, nutritional care aspects by using pictorial posters, charts, CDs in local language. Importance of balanced diet, low cost nutritious foods, nutritional deficiencies, diet during illness, regular health checkups were given to the experimental group.

Strategies used for intervention

1. Infants were given stimulation programme based on the developmental level. Different activities for different age group of infants were planned.
2. Mothers of infant babies were given education about stimulation , health and nutritional care by using audio-visual aids
3. Adolescents were given life skill education by planning sessions for each sub dimension of life skills .simple exercises, dramatization, simulatory sessions were planned for better understanding.
4. Overall life satisfaction was measured before and after intervention from the farm women

Post – test

After implementation of intervention programme for period of 6 months using the standardized intervention packages and structured infant stimulation programme, the impact of the intervention programmes in improving the knowledge levels of rural mothers and adolescents and developmental status of infants was done after the intervention. To measure the quality of life of rural women, life satisfaction scale was used after the intervention programme. The pre and post test scores were analysed using appropriate statistical methods.

Statistical analysis

The pre test and post test data collected from rural mothers, infants, adolescents and farm women was analysed by using both descriptive and inferential statistics. Frequencies and percentages, mean and standard deviation were used to assess the knowledge levels of participants. Inferential statistics were t-test, correlation analysis to study the significant difference between independent and dependent variables.

Results and Discussion

Socio- Demographic Profile of the Sample

As a first step the socio-demographic profile of sample is presented. The distribution of sample according to age, family income, and educational status.

Table-1: Demographic Profile of the Sample (n=30)

S. No	Mother Variables		Number	Per cent (%)
1	Age in years	20-25	20	67
		26-30	10	33
		Total	**30**	**100**
2	Income level	High	7	7
		Middle	19	63
		Low	9	30
		Total	**30**	**100**
3	Educational status	Below 5th class	5	17
		5-10th class	16	53
		Higher degree	9	30
		Total	**30**	**100**

Table-1 Indicates that 67 %of sample fall in the age group of 20-25 years and 33 %are from 26-30 years. When the family income considered 63 %families have middle income next to 30 %had low income families and 7 %families were from high income level. Nearly half of the sample 53 %had education up to 10th class and 30 %sample were completed their college education few sample 17 %were completed primary education.

Table -2 Distribution of Infants according to the Gender and Age

S.No	Infant child Variables	Number
1	**Gender**	
	Boys	10(34%)
	Girls	20(66%)
2	**Age in months**	
	Below 6 months	6(20%)
	7 -12 months	10 (33%)
	14 months to 17 months	3(10%)
	18 months to 24 months	9(30%)
	25 months to 29 months	2(7%)

Table-2 shows the distribution of sample according to gender and age. The sample selected included 34 % of boys and 66 %of girls. Thirty three % of sample fall in the age group of 7-12 months, 30 %were from 18 months to 24 months, 20 % of sample were below 6 months, 10 %of sample in the age group of above 12 months and 7 %were above 2 years of age.

Table-3 indicates that 50 % of the sample were boys and 50 % were girls and 40 % of the sample were in the age group of 13 years and 60 %were 14 years.

Table-3 Distribution of sample according of the Adolescents Gender and age

S.No	Adolescent Variables	Number
1	Gender	
	Boys	15(50%)
	Girls	15(50%)
2	Age	
	13 years	12(40%)
	14 years	18(60%)

Existing practices of child care in the village

Health care

- Most of the women(75%)are going to hospitals for their delivery.
- All the mothers opined that feeding colostrum after delivery is important for the health of the new born.
- All mothers were found to have good knowledge regarding vaccines.

Nutritional care

- All women expressed that eating papaya and sesame seeds during their pregnancy period generate heat and causes abortion.

- Majority of the mothers (76 %) are giving weaning foods after 8-9 months. The common weaning foods given include – Mixed cereal grain powder, curd rice, biscuits, smashed banana

Traditional and cultural restrictions

- Pregnant women are not allowed to go out during solar/ lunar eclipse and no moon day It was told that some food restrictions are alsoobserved.

The common restrictions believed are

1. Not using any sharp object such as a knife, scissors or a needle during eclipse
2. Not eating anything till the eclipse is completed.
3. Resting as much as possible during the eclipse time
4. Covering the windows with newspaper or thick curtains so that no rays of the eclipse enter the home.
5. Throwing away all cooked food and water after the eclipse.
6. Taking bath after the eclipse time .

Child rearing practices

- Hundred %of farm mothers have knowledge about breastfeeding practices
- The pregnant, lactating mothers with infants aged 6–24 months are registered with the local 'Anganwadi' centres.
- Immunization is followed as per the schedule.
- Traditional health care practices like pouring oil into nose and ears, applying turmeric on the skull to control cold , giving castor oil for easy motions or stomach ache, giving omum water for improving digestion, giving vaza for early development of language etc are still practiced in

the village.

Table -4 shows the distribution of farm women on nutritional knowledge. At pre-test, majority of farm women (57%) had low level of knowledge related to nutrition aspects and 43 %of farm women had medium level of nutritional knowledge. After the nutrition education intervention given for farm women, post test results revealed that majority of mothers of infants (83%) had good knowledge of nutrition and 10 % had medium level of nutritional level. The strategies used for giving intervention were nutrition education, promoting nutritional garden and enriching the diets with low cost nutritious foodsThus, intervention was found to be effective for mothers of infant babies in improving the knowledge levels of rural mothers.

Table-4 Knowledge levels of farm women on Nutrition component (pre and post test) n=30

S.No	Nutritional knowledge level	Pre test	Post test
1	High level	0 (0)	27(90%)
2	Medium level	13(43%)	3(10%)
3	Low level	17(57%)	0(0)

Table 5 indicates that during the pretest sixty percent of farm women were not aware of the importance of balanced diet during pregnancy whereas thirty %were aware of balanced diet. After conducting intervention programme for 6 months awareness about the low cost foods and balanced diet was improved. During the post-test it was observed that 86 %of farm women were aware of importance of balanced diet during pregnancy whereas 14 %were not aware.

Table-5 Awareness levels of farm women on importance of balanced diet n=30

S.No	Variable	Pre test		Post test	
1	Balanced diet	Aware	Not aware	Aware	Not aware
		40%	60%	86%	14%

There was a significant difference found in the pre and post intervention scores in the area of nutrition. Mothers of infants could comprehend well about the feeding practices and low cost weaning foods for the children. Their knowledge about the balanced diet and nutrients was also increased during post test.

Table 6: Comparison of Nutritional scores pre & post intervention. N=30

Variables	Mean &S.D Nutrition scores	P-value
Pre-intervention	15.03(0.26)	6.15*
Post-intervention	20.5(0.14)	

Table 7shows the distribution of farm women on health knowledge pre and post-test. At pre-test, majority of farm women (80) had high level of knowledge related to health like taking TT injection during pregnancy and immunizing child after birth. 20% of farm women had medium level of health knowledge. After the health education intervention given for farm women , post test results revealed that majority of mothers of infants (90%) had high of knowledge of nutrition and 10 % had medium level of nutritional level. The strategies used for giving intervention were through reproductive and child health education, Demonstrations and group discussions on scientific child rearing practices, Infant stimulation, Immunization . Thus, intervention was found to be effective for mothers of infant babies in improving the knowledge level of mothers of infant babies similar studies supported. Shamila Hamid in North Kashmir (2011), found that more than half of the of the mothers 184 (61.3%) had good knowledge regarding vaccines.

Table-7 Knowledge levels of farm women on health component pre and post test

S.No	Health level	Pre test	Post test
1	High level	24(80%)	27(90%)
2	Medium level	6(20%)	3(10%)
3	Low level	-	-

Life skills development of adolescent

Table 8: Comparison of life skills scores pre &post intervention. N=30

Variables	Mean & S.D life skills scores	t-value
Pre-intervention	115.53 (1.22)	6.77*
Post-intervention	177.73 (0.787)	

Figure-3 shows the competencies of adolescents in life skills. Before intervention, majority of adolescent had poor life skills scores (83.33%). After the educational intervention, results revealed that majority of adolescents had high life skills scores (76.66 %) and 23.34% had middle level life skills scores. Thus, intervention was found to be effective among adolescents to develop and enhance their life skills. The results of Sharma (2003) are also in line with these findings indicating that after the life skill intervention programme majority of the adolescents (51%) improved life skills as compared to before.

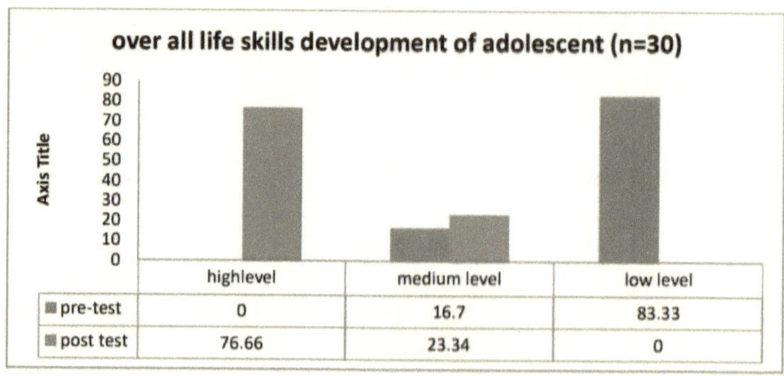

	highlevel	medium level	low level
pre-test	0	16.7	83.33
post test	76.66	23.34	0

Fig.3. Over all Life skills development of adolescents

The findings are also supported by Nejad (2010) who found that Life skills training is an effective prevention method for adolescents experiencing a wide variety of mental, emotional, behavioural, and physical problems.

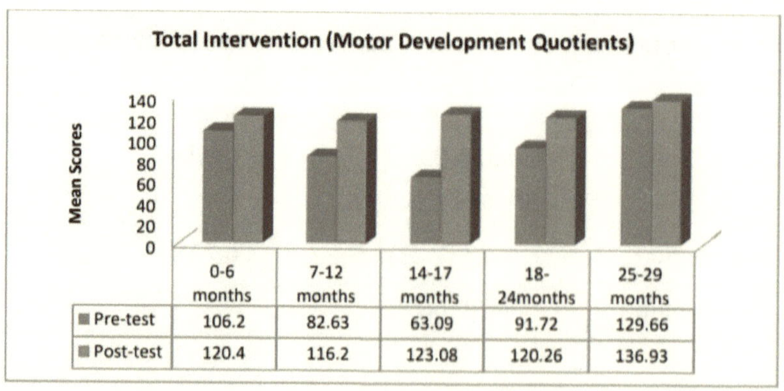

	0-6 months	7-12 months	14-17 months	18-24months	25-29 months
Pre-test	106.2	82.63	63.09	91.72	129.66
Post-test	120.4	116.2	123.08	120.26	136.93

Fig no 4: Mean scores of motor and mental development of rural infants

This education brings up the sense of qualification, capacity of being effective, ability to deal with defeating problems, objective and rational approaches to the problem. Life skills programmes are comprehensive and include various areas like thinking, behaviour and emotions to achieve a healthy life

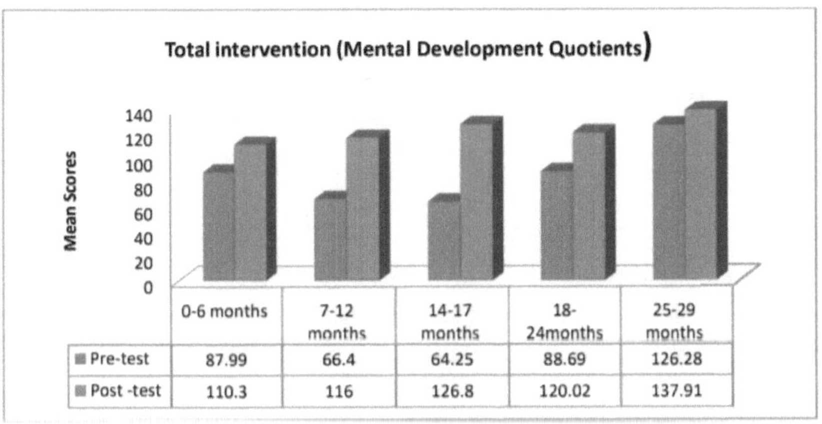

	0-6 months	7-12 months	14-17 months	18-24months	25-29 months
Pre-test	87.99	66.4	64.25	88.69	126.28
Post -test	110.3	116	126.8	120.02	137.91

Fig no 5: Mean scores of motor and mental development of rural infants

Motor development Intervention

Motor intervention was given to the children for six months using educational intervention package coupled with motor stimulatory activities. The post test scores in all the age groups of children indicated a significant improvement in the motor development scores compared to pre test scores.

Mental development Intervention

Child's mental development was assessed during pre test using DASII and based on the mental age score developmental intervention was given to the mother and child using the intervention package and stimulatory activities.

Child's mental development was found to be improved significantly during the post-test.

Table 9: Comparison of mean motor development quotients (pre & post intervention) N=30

Variables	Mean &S.D Motor development quotients	t- value
Pre-intervention	90.28 (4.71)	
Post-intervention	120.28 (4,677)	4.51*

A significant difference found in the intervention scores in the area of motor development. Mothers of infants could comprehend well about the infant stimulation and low cost material preparation of toys for the children.

Table 10: Comparison of mean mental developmental quotients (pre & post intervention) N=30

Variables	Mean &S.D mental development quotients	t-value
Pre-intervention	82.73 (5.15)	6.51*
Post-intervention	118 (3.554)	

A significant difference found in the intervention scores in the area of mental development. Mothers of infants could comprehend well about the infant stimulation and low cost material preparation of toys for the children.

Life satisfaction of farm women

There was a significant difference found between the pre and post test scores in the life satisfaction component of farm families. The integrated strategic interventions given for a period of six months in the areas of health, nutrition, infant stimulation and life skills education to the mothers of infants and adolescent girls has increases their competencies and confidence levels. The increased scores of life satisfaction indicate a better quality of life.

Table:11   Life Satisfaction scores (Pre and Post test) N=30

Variables	Mean &S.D life satisfaction	t-value
Pre-intervention	79.56 (22.35)	7.18*
Post-intervention	127.53 (3.88)	

From the above figure it is evident that majority of the women (63%) were scored low on the life satisfaction scale during pre-test and 30 %women had medium levels of life satisfaction. The women farmers were given interventions to improve their knowledge and skills in the areas of health, nutrition and infant stimulation activities for a period of six months using standardized intervention packages.

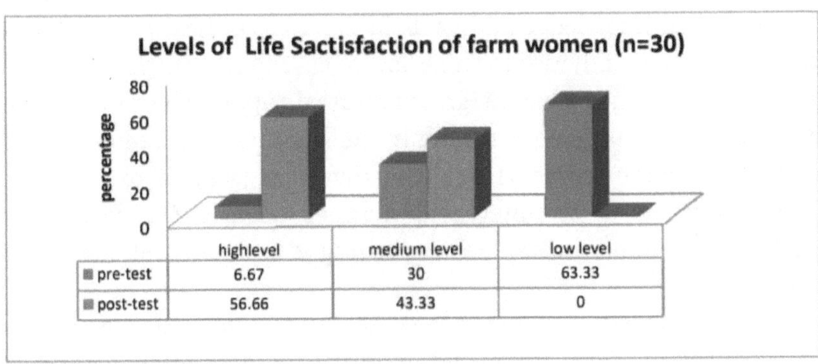

Fig 8: Levels of Life Satisfaction of farm women

Similarly adolescent boys and girls of farm families were given life skills education to improve their competencies in different areas. This integrated approach of interventions had worked out to be good resulting in the significant increase in the post test life satisfaction scores. The post test scores indicate that 56.6% of women farmers fell in the high level category of life satisfaction and 43.3% reported medium levels of life satisfaction. Similar findings are being supported by Luke Fortney, Charlene, Larissa and Aleksandra, David (2012) participants had improvement compared the post intervention they had significantly better scores .where it was stated that integrated interventions help in improving the life satisfaction of the individuals and thereby improving the quality of life.

Conclusion

The study concluded that Majority of the infants during the pre –test had less mental scores compared to post test. The increase in the scores during post-test was due to the developmental intervention given to the infant mothers to improve the mental and motor skills of infants through stimulation activities. Similarly mothers had low levels of knowledge on nutrition and health issues at the initial stages and the scores improved after intervention.

Most of the women were scored low on the life satisfaction scale during pre-test. The women farmers were given integrated strategic interventions to improve their knowledge and skills in the areas of health, nutrition and infant stimulation activities for a period of six months using standardized intervention packages. This integrated strategic approach of interventions had worked out to be good resulting in the significant increase in the post test life satisfaction scores. Hence it is always suggestible to provide and plan intervention in an integrated manner using a standardized and suitable intervention model for improving the quality of life of farm families.

Similarly the study concluded that the rural adolescents who had little knowledge about life skills did improve better after intervention programme. Life skill education is very important for adolescents as now a days there is more influence of mass media and mobile phones. Rural adolescents lack social cognitive skills, problem solving and decision making skills which are essential as soon they will be entering into family life.

The study highlights the importance of integrated interventions for better quality life. Many intervention studies were taken up in the rural context which focuses on only one component like either health, nutrition or developmental intervention or life skills focussing on one age group of family. This type of approach does not really works in providing better quality of life.

Instead if the intervention is planned for all the age groups of the family members to suit their needs the outcome will be effective. The strategies used in the study include – educating the participants by using the audio-visual materials, CDs, short films, demonstrations, simulation exercises. All these approaches are useful especially when we are dealing with uneducated people.

References

1. Aparna.N and Raakhee.A.S. (2001). Life Skill Education for Adolescents and Its Relevance and Importance, Educational Science and Psychology, Vol-21

2. Christine Helfrich, A. and Louis Fogg L. (2007). Outcomes of a Life Skills Intervention for Homeless Adults. The journal of Primary Prevention . Volume 28(3) .PP 13-326 .

3. Chhabra, R., & Rokx, C. (2004). The nutrition MDG indicator: interpreting progress. Health, Nutrition, and Population (HNP) discussion paper. W. Bank. Washington, D.C., the International Bank for Reconstruction and Development, The World Bank.

4. Dharmalingam, A., Navaneetham, K., and Krishnakumar, C.S. (2010).Nutritional status of mothers and low birth weight in India. Maternal and Child Health, 14(2): 290-298.

5. Gupta, A. and N. S. Khaira (2008). Flaws in Child Nutrition and Health Governance. Economic and Political Weekly.Mumbai.43: 5.

6. Karri Sisson (2015). in her working paper on effectiveness of strategic interventions to improve the quality of life of rural families.) Discussion Paper; Prioritizing Nutrition in Agriculture and Rural Development: Guiding Principles for Operational Investments.The World Bank, Washington DC.

7. Rohinipandcy ,Kathcleen and Sukanya (2014). Improving the reproductive health and nutrition status of married and unmarried

youth.Journal of marriage and family welfare.12(4).49-522.

8. Nejad, S.Y.M.Y., (2010). The Impact of Life Skills Training onSelf-esteem, Mental Health, and Assertiveness: A Study among Students of Boosher's High Schooling Iran. Department of Psychology, University of Kerala

9. Sandhya.K., and Shivani. K. (2012). Life skills of Adolescents in relation to their Self-concept developed through Yuva School Life Skill Programme, International Journal of Social Sciences and interdisciplinary Research, Vol.1(11):115-125.

10. Samuels, B. and Anderson, C. (2014). Integration of nutrition and health for targeted outcomes.Health action .Vol. 32 (2).20-24.

11. Saxena, N. C. (2009). Call to action: Hunger, under-nutrition, and food security in India. Policy brief series. New Delhi, Centre for Legislative Research and Advocacy (CLRA): 8.

12. Singh, P., & Joseph, G. (1996). Manual for Life Satisfaction Scale. Agra, India: National Psychological Corporation

13. Srinivasan K, C Shekhar, et al. (2007). Reviewing Reproductive and Child Health Programmes in India.Economic& Political Weekly. 42: 2931-2939.

14. Teneja.V ,Beri.R.S and Puliyal J.M (2014). Play in orphanages Indian journal of paediatrics vol71

15. UNICEF (2006). Progress for children - A report card on nutrition. New York: New York. Available online at: http://www.unicef.org/publications/ files/Progress_for_Children_- No._4.pdf

16. Victora, CG, Adair, L, Fall, C, Hallal, PC, Martorell, R, et al. (2008). Maternal and child under nutrition: consequences for adult health and human capital. Lancet, 371(9609): 340- 357.

17. White H. (2005). Comment on contributions regarding the impact of the Bangladesh Integrated Nutrition Project. Health Policy and Planning, 20(6):408-411.

X

Preparing for the Future: Integration of Life Skills and Spiritual Intelligence in ECCE Curriculum

Manisha Dhami[1], Neha Joshi[1], Seema Sharma[2]
[1]Research Scholar, [2]Principal Extension Scientist
Human Development & Family Studies
Punjab Agricultural University, Ludhiana-141001
Email Id: manisha-hd@pau.edu

Abstract

India is home to the largest child population in the world and has population of 16.45 Cr children in the age group 0-6 years (Census 2011). The initial six years of a child's life is extremely sensitive phase for overall development and the experiences child gets during these years have long-lasting impact on his/ her personality. Children have pertinent role in the society as today's children are the hope, future citizen and leaders of tomorrow. ECCE has prospect to nurture caring, capable and responsible future adults. Quality of early childhood care and learning experiences in home and school to which young children are exposed lay foundation for preparing a ready child. The ECCE curriculum is trying hard to inculcate basic domains of development of the child and more emphasis on academics is always a priority but the psycho-social competencies are still missing. The ECCE programs need to be resolute by children's developmental, personal and contextual needs, intending for more need based inputs and an enabling environment. Integration of life skills program and spiritual intelligence education in the ECCE curriculum have potential to make significant contribution in promoting psycho-social competencies of young children which have important role in later life also. Evidences of research showed that young children with basic life skills have propensity to be more confident and competent. With a strong foundation of literacy skills and profusion of valuable life skills, children become able young adults who are passably prepared for successful future. There is much focus on the development of the cognitive, social and emotional dimensions of preschoolers as a part of their school readiness, the spiritual dimension is often brushed over or ignored totally. The spiritual intelligence creates responsive behaviour towards ourselves, family, society, our surrounding, our country and universe. It makes connection of personal vision with the larger good of humanity. Thus, there is a need to incorporate life skill and spiritual intelligence dimension in the educational curriculum of early childhood education.

Keywords: Early childhood, Psycho-social competencies, Curriculum, Life skills, Spiritual intelligence

Introduction

The outlook of every society is based on its capacity of promoting the growth and development of the young generation. As stated simply, the present day children will become tomorrow's citizens, workers, and parents. The initial years of individual's lives, defined as the early childhood period, have significance for the vigorous growth and development in the later life. Generally, time period of prenatal period to six years of age is known as early childhood, moreover it's a significant stage for brain development in the whole lifespan (UNICEF, 2012). These initial years are very critical period impacting all the developmental spheres of children for entire life. India has the largest child population (16.45 Cr) in the age group of 0-6 years around the globe (Census 2011). Erikson (1950) stated that during this stage child gain autonomy, discover to make choice and acknowledge the consequences of choice. In this stage of life, one's development can be given a lending hand for reaching the maximum potential and determines what one's personality will be (Hurlock, 1978).

Considering this, early childhood education aims to attain optimal growth and development among young children lying in the age bar of birth to six years by using educational stimulus that helps in developing school readiness for smooth transition to formal education (National Education System, 2003). *ECCE has the opportunity of rearing and caring of skilled and responsible future adults.* Besides creating a foundation for linguistic and cognitive competencies, it also encourages crucial psycho-social development of youngsters. Children learn many things during these significant years. Education during early childhood guides an important base for children's learning. Hence, it should be a vital part of the whole education system. The goal of furnishing universal admittance to quality pre-primary education is an accessible objective that needs an efficient and practical approach to deals with present situation.

Quality of pre-primary education

Provision of providing quality early education is an excellent investments for assuring the forthcoming accomplishment of today's kids. Universal pre-primary education of superior quality will lead to massive benefits to young children, families, education systems, as well as society in whole. Kids exposed to quality early schooling are better equipped for the successful transition to formal education. Nevertheless, failure in offering quality early childhood education restrict children's later success by refusing their prospect to accomplish complete potential (UNICEF, 2019). It also curbs the future of countries, robbing their chance to diminish inequalities and endorse peace along with prosperous communities. Researchers have made effort to assess the quality parameters for ensuring distinction in early childhood education. It has been observed that quality early childhood education depends on the physical environment and materials along with teachers' competencies, classroom strength, the child–teacher ratio, teacher-child interactions, core curriculum, parental involvement (Epinosa, 2002). Thus, it could be concluded that the preschool setting, an output of micro, meso and macro systems of ecological theory, is considered to be have indispensable role in child's preparation for a self-satisfied life that could be enhanced through the integration of Life Skills and Spiritual intelligence program in its curriculum.

Life Skills Education

Life skills are essential competencies for young children to grow up to be active and creative individuals resulting in responsible and independent adult. According to WHO (1997), life skills are positive and adaptive behavioral abilities that support a person to effectively deal with demands and challenges during his life. The Kenya Institute of Education (2008) defined life skills as the competencies acquires by the individual for efficient adaptation and for dealing with the demands of daily life. A life skill is defined as a kind of practical guidance helping an individual to learn how to care for the body, grow to be an individual, work with other people, make logical decisions, protects them to achieve goals in their lives.

Basic life skills are important for young children that can be learned in the early years of life includes self-awareness, empathy, decision making, problem-solving, resilience, creative thinking, communication, collaboration, and conflict resolution skills (Akfirat & Kezer, 2016). These skills motivate children by helping them to understand themselves and their potential in their lives so that they can arrange life goals and conduct problem-solving processes when faced with life problems. Life-oriented education can be provided at various levels of education including the preschool level. Based on the characteristics of early childhood development, life skills are tailored to the level of child development that is generally still in preoperational thinking.

A life skills program is a practical approach for the growth of preschoolers in numerous ways targeting the cognitive as well as socio-emotional domains of development. The probable outcomes for the young children admitted in this program are development of required qualities like self-confidence, benevolence, acceptance and responsibility (Ferrari *et al.*, 2004; Goody, 2001). Life Skills curriculum development aims to stimulate a number of abilities and skills that must be possessed by a child to be able to live their lives. Hence, life skills education is understood as edification that provides personal, social life skills, skills aimed at developing children's abilities. This life skills curriculum is structured by designing a play activity program which is a set of learning experiences through play that will be provided to children in the context of achieving competence based on developmental tasks that must be mastered. For the Life Skill Program to be prolific and have an optimistic influence on young children, the program must be fastened on a viewpoint that highlights the mutual and dynamic interaction among individuals and community (Edelstein, 2010). Life skills can be introduced to children through habituation by the cultural background in the place of residence. Overall, life skills education has observed to be an efficient psychosocial mediation approach for encouraging positive social, and mental health of an individual which had a crucial function in many facets like improved coping strategies, better self-confidence and higher emotional intelligence along with efficient critical thinking, problem-solving and decision-making skills (Ramesh & Farshad, 2004). Thus, it is worth to integrate life skill education into the traditional early childhood curriculum and should be given by a trained educator to boost the socio-emotional development of children and equipping them with better-adapted proficiency to confront the difficulties of the formal school setting in later years. Thus, it could be concluded that competencies (personal, thinking, and social skills) addressed by the Life Skills Programme are key for children's school readiness for smooth transition from kindergarten to formal educational setup (Kokkalia *et al* 2019).

Spiritual Intelligence based Education

Most of the time, the general emphasis is on the physical, emotional, cognitive, and social development of the children, often the spiritual dimension goes missing completely (Hyde, 2009). Spiritual intelligence tends to address numerous ways of knowing and for the integration of the inner life of mind and spirit with the outer life of work in the world. Spiritual intelligence is referred as an ability with which human can have access to deepest meanings, purpose, and motivation (Zohar, 2005; Marshal, 2000) Spiritual intelligence Spiritual intelligence should be address without delay as it is pertinent for insight in creating spiritual choices which add to the psychological well-being and on the complete vigorous human development. (Nakagawa, 2009).

Education-based on spiritual intelligence will help children in generating these following traits:

a. **Self awareness:** It aims to identify what individual care about and what they live for. The main feature of it is to live true and authentic to oneself while obliging others. This helps individuals to connect with our deeper self.

b. **Spontaneity:** It helps individuals for being responsive for their actions at time.

c. **Holism:** It guide person to realize that they are the part of identical system. It facilitates cooperation, connection and offers a sense of belonging.

d. **Compassion:** It is emotional response; a feeling and thought embraced the desire to help.

e. **Celebration of diversity:** It allows celebrating our differences because they make us learn what really matters. It helps people to think in different perspective of diversity where new neurons find connection and growth.

f. **Field Independence:** It means "to stand against the crowd" and follow their own convictions.

g. **Humility:** it is pertinent dimension to go parallel with field independence, where individual realizes the sense of being a player in a play and able to ask themselves that Am I right to think what I do? Did I listened to all the arguments against it? Have I thought deeply about it?

h. **Propensity to ask fundamental 'why?' questions:** It help individuals to develop logical thinking and allows them to comprehend effects and get under deep level of understanding.

a. **Potential to Reframe: It allows human to think beyond the problem and look for larger picture.**

j. **Positive use of adversity**: It is all about identifying, accepting, and acknowledging their own mistakes, setbacks and sufferings. It gives learning that sufferings are inevitable in human life; they give pain yet can make human more wise, brave and strong.

k. **Sense of vocation**: It appeals to person with larger good of humanity, it's a sense to serve society and give back something. (Zohar,2005)

In the present educational context, the spiritual dimension of children should not be unnoticed as it can make children more resilient, help to reduce anxiety, escalate their mental horizon and off course refurbish the equilibrium between head and heart. It gives pure awareness and is identical to the endless reality that has immense compassion.

A proper schedule could be fixed in the timetable of the educational curriculum for practicing skills/ qualities like affection, empathy, warmth, caring, and kindness for children. Children are the future of world and have the higher duties of creating the wise human capital of the nation. Children need to develop superior qualities as having an important role in nation-building. The young mind should get nourishment with higher abilities. Thus, integrating spiritual intelligence into the educational curriculum can be proved as a blessing to meet the challenges in particular and humanity in general.

Strategies to integrate Life Skills and Spiritual Intelligence in ECCE curriculum

According to Bandura (1986), Children always observe, imitate and model the behaviors of others and from here the learning occurs. The interplay between child and their environment decide a lot about their behavior ,whereas, Piaget (2000) agreed that children aren't passive receptors and highlighted that participation in meaningful activities are only the way to build build schema and learn about new concept. Later findings by Dewey (2001) stated that children learning can be achieved by doing and living. Thus, educational curriculum should match the children interest, , abilities, natural characteristics, and individual differences. He also bring point that children should not be enforced into a passive and rote learning based educational curriculum. Rather than this, actual education must focus on practical experiences instead of theory. Children must be provided with enormous opportunities to explore, discover and built cognition. It is very important to merge experiential learning with combined experience, perception, cognition, and behavior and permit children to explore, create an experience and monitor their learning outcomes (Loo, 2004).

Keeping these theoretical perspectives in consideration, the preschool curriculum, as well as teachers plays a critical role in enhancing life skills and spiritual intelligence among young ones. Their main focus should be deliberately creating a web of activities that motivate children to practice life skills and spirituality in their daily routine life. Various activities used to inculcate life skills and spiritual intelligence in the curriculum of early childhood education could be through employing personal growth activities, eco-environment approach, reading stories, role plays, digital videos, brainstorming, concept mapping, discussion, and various spiritual practices including prayers yoga meditation, psychotherapy or mystical experiences.

In general, developing positive psychology in young children has a remarkable impact on their skills and abilities to experience their lives and face emerging challenges (Shoshani & Slone, 2017). Some of the practices employed by teachers in a pre-school setting to gain and develop basic life skills and spiritual intelligence among young children include activities for self-reflection, creating a democratic and positive learning environment for role modeling, nurturing creativity, encourage the participation of kids in small level social welfare project, encouraging group learning, recognition, and celebration of kids accomplishment of psycho-social learning as well as encouraging participation and collaboration of family and community as a whole for younger's learning. Furthermore, to enhance the spiritual intelligence among young children, teachers require to support and engages with every child in a positive way in the form of warmth, approval, and positive expressions (Wahyuningsih, 2018).

Practical strategies that could be used to enhance the life skills and spiritual intelligence among young children include:

- Plan experiences through art activities like role play, mime, drawing, craft and music helpful for enabling kids to develop self-awareness.
- Ask young ones to label feelings and also to focus on others so that feeling of compassion and empathy develops.
- Let them offer chance to utilize journals that could help children to connect and engage with meaning and value. It could be a worthy way for kids to work through and eloquent their thoughts and feelings
- Create the environment for solitude and silence through a classroom programme enabling children to connect with subject of meaning and value.
- Take advantage of quiet places like outdoor garden area, multi-purpose rooms, or school premises for calm reflection among young ones.
- Read, perceive and interpret and disseminate stories where individuals have been competent to use their life skills and spiritual intelligence using teaching methods.
- Offer opportunities for children to develop connection in apparently varied things and it could be accomplished in numerous subject arenas that would be specifically useful as a part of an integrated approach to curriculum.

- Students must be taught to value every moment and event of life, and offer them to give opportunities to experience what may portray to be common routine and boring things.
- Plan to edify them about meticulous qualities, such as compassion, empathy, hope, interpersonal skills, and coping skills through dissemination of tales or through various art forms. Just telling and teaching children about such virtues doesn't essentially denote that children will gain competence for them until it is not experienced by children themselves and made explicit.

Conclusions

Preschool education is most important section for the growth and development of young ones. It occupies children with skills, knowledge and provides them a gateway into formal schooling and success in later years of life. Keeping this in consideration, New Education Policy also considers that ECCE ideally should consist of flexible, versatile, creative, play and fun based, and inquiry-based learning concept via puzzles, critical thinking, problem-solving, art and craft, role play, puppetry, music and movement. The main focus of NEP 2020 at the pre-primary level is to create and develop social skills like ethical behavior, courtesy, sensitivity, personal and community hygiene, teamwork, collaboration and cooperation.

Thus, it could be deducted from numerous studies is that promoting and inculcating life skills and spiritual intelligence in preschool level can structure a foundation of envisaging how deftly children can carry out at later schooling and in their future. The implications of spiritual intelligence and life skills training for children during early years contribute to the development of character, emotional, psychological, and physical aspects. Thus it could be concluded that teaching Life Skills and Spiritual intelligence-based ECCE curriculum to preschool children paves their way for schooling and social responsibilities (Gatumu & Kathuri, 2018).

References

1. Akfirat, O. N., & Kezer, F. (2016). A Program Implementation for the Development of Life Skills of Primary School 4th Grade Students. *Journal*

of Education and Practice, 7(35), 9-16.

2. Bandura, A. (1986). *Social foundations of thought and action: a social cognitive theory.* Pp. 23-28. Englewood Cliffs, NJ: Prentice-Hall.

3. Dewey, J. (2001). *Democracy and education.* State College: The Pennsylvania State University, A Penn State Electronic Classics Series Publication.

4. Edelstein, S. (2010). *Life cycle nutrition: an evidence-based approach.* Jones & Bartlett Publishers, Burlington.

5. Epinosa, L.M. (2002). *High-quality preschool: Why we need it and what it looks like. Preschool Policy Matters.* National Institute for Early Education Research.

6. Ferrari, T. M., Hogue, C. A., and Scheer, S. D. (2004). Parents' perceptions of life skills development in the 4-H cloverbud program. *Journal of Extension,* 42(3).

7. Gatumu, J. C., &and Kathuri, W. N. (2018). An Exploration of Life Skills Programme on Pre-School Children in Embu West, Kenya. *Journal of Curriculum and Teaching,* 7(1), 1-6.

8. Goody, J. (2001). Competencies and education: Contextual diversity. Defining and selecting key competencies. In Rychen, D. S. E., & Salganik, L. H. E. (Eds). *Defining and selecting key competencies.* Pp. 175-190. Hogrefe & Huber Publishers.

9. Hurlock E (1978). *Child Development.* McGraw-Hill Book Company, New York.

10. **Hyde, B. (2009). Spiritually intelligent kids: Children using SQ to enhance holistic learning and wellbeing. In *International handbook of education for spirituality, care and wellbeing.* Pp. 855-871. Springer, Dordrecht.**

11. Kenya Institute of Education. (2008). *Early Childhood Development and Education Syllabus.* Kenya Institute of Education, Nairobi.

12. Kokkalia, G., Drigas, A., Economou, A., & Roussos, P. (2019). School Readiness from Kindergarten to Primary School. *International Journal of Emerging Technologies in Learning,* 14(11), 4.

13. Loo, R. (2004). Kolb's learning styles and learning preferences: Is there a linkage? *Educational Psychology,* 24(1), 99–108.

14. Marshall. (2000). *SQ: Spiritual Intelligence*: The Ultimate Intelligence. Bloomsbury, New York

15. Nakagawa, Y. (2009). Awareness and compassion for the education of enlightenment. In *International handbook of education for spirituality, care and wellbeing.* Pp. 593-609. Dordrecht, Springer.

16. National Education System. (2003). Act of The Republic of Indonesia, No. 20.

17. Piaget, J. (2000). *Çocukta zihinsel gelişim*. In H. Portakal (Ed.), Trans. Cem Yayınevi: İstanbul.

18. Ramesht, M., & Farshad, C. (2009). Study of life skills training in prevention of drug abuse in students. Pp. 70-2. In *Third seminar of students' mental health*, Iran University of Science and Technology; Persian.

19. Shoshani, A., & Slone, M. (2017). Positive education for young children: effects of a positive psychology intervention for preschool children on subjective well being and learning behaviors. *Frontiers in psychology, 8*, 1866.

20. **UNICEF (2019) *A World Ready to Learn: Prioritizing quality early childhood education.* UNICEF. Retrieved from https://data.unicef.org/resources/a-world-ready-to-learn-report/.**

21. **Wahyuningsih, S. (2018). Promoting children's spiritual intelligence and personality development. *Jurnal Penelitian*, 189-201.**

22. **Zohar, D. (2005). What is Spiritual Intelligence?. *Journal of Humanistic Psychology*, 42; 2: 16–33.**

XI

Radio Frequency Identification (RFID) Technology in Fashion & Retail

Shalini Mohanty[1], Avni Singhal[2], Prarthana Kapadia[3]
[1]Assistant Professor, [2]Student - M. Design, [3]Student - B. Design
School of Fashion Design & Technology,
Amity University, Mumbai
Email Id: 1mohanty.shalini@gmail.com

Abstract

What began its journey in the mid-20th century as a major spy device developed by Leon Theremin for the Soviet Government during World War - II, has now successfully carved its place in the fashion world as one of the most productive and efficient technology. With 73%of the fashion and retail industry using Radio Frequency Identification (RFID) Technology somewhere within their respective business models, it's safe to say that RFID is not only one of the most omnipotent and widely used technologies in the industry but it is also the most promising one in terms of its prospective growth and evolution in its usage. Known for majorly improving supply-chain management via minimisation of loss of inventory, increasing productivity and agility of activities, and enhancement of product or stock info precision, RFID technology alleviates any discrepancies that may lead to losses in businesses. With these characteristics in mind, this article is a curation of wide spread applications of RFID, from "inventory management, production control, retail management, and brand segregation," to sustainability in the fashion and retail industry. Additionally, the challenges and prospective evolution of RFID technology in the fashion and retail industry will also be discussed and extrapolated.

Keywords: RFID, Radio Frequency Identification Technology, Inventory Management, Retail Management, Production Control, Sustainability

Introduction to RFID Technology

Zougar (2018, para 1) states that RFID is the acronym for "Radio-Frequency Identification". A technology based on the radio-waves that automatically recognise the information in the tags through devices. An 'antenna' and a 'microchip' are used to send and collect data on an RFID tag. Three basic components used to characterise this technology are: "the chip, the antenna, and the reader." (Zougar, 2018, para 2)

The operation of RFID systems is dependent on the transmission of electromagnetic waves over a long distance. The signals are sent on a specific frequency by the reader to either one or more tags in its reading area, which responds with a signal of their own. The label is fed by the electromagnetic field, which triggers the chip. (Zougar, 2018, para 3)

Certain magnitude or phase modulation is generated by the tag on the carrier frequency to transmit the details contained in the chip. When the reader receives this content, it converts the information to binary code. In the other direction, the operation remains symmetrical. (Zougar, 2018, para 4)

The procedure for radio frequency detection is as follows, and shown in Diagram 1:

- To activate the tag, the reader transmits energy via radio.
- It looks up tags in the area.
- It attends the responses & removes the duplicates or response to repetitions.
- And lastly, it forwards the obtained outcome to the appropriate approach.

(Zougar, 2018, para 5)

RFID tags/chips receive a radio signal or respond with a different signal immediately which contains any relevant data. A microcircuit and an antenna are included in each tag. The scanning is done with a reader that recognises the radio frequency signals coming from the RFID tags, comparable to how a barcode is read with an optical laser. (Zougar, 2018, para 6)

There are 3 types of RFID tags and they are shown in and shown in Diagram too:

- Passive tags: These do not require any power source other than the provided by readers at the time of the scan.
- Active tags: These are the gadgets having batteries and can also communicate with the readers. Its frequency can also be measured from long distance unlike passive tags.
- Semi-active tags: These tags can be used for communication like passive tags and the battery is used to record the data only.

(Zougar, 2018, para 9)

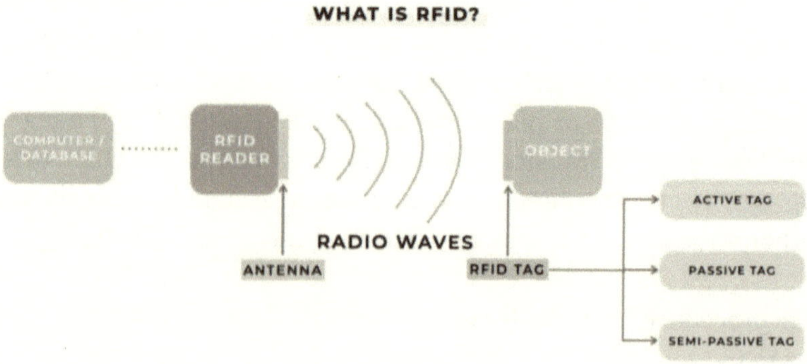

Figure1: RFID and types of RFID Tags.

The main features of any RFID tag are:

- It has a huge storage capacity.
- Scanner reading ranges from a few centimetres to about 200 meters
- May not necessarily be written. However, the label can be re-written and recycled.
- Easy usability.

(Zougar, 2018, para 10)

According to the capacity of the installation and the radio waves used, the frequency has a distance of a few hundred metres. The frequency of a radio wave is measured in Hertz (Hz) or repetitions per second and can be further classified as:

- Low frequency - These frequencies range from 30 and 300 kHz, with wavelengths of 1 to 10 km and playback distances of 10cm. The acronym LF is used in RFID to represent a tag that uses low frequency (Low Frequency) & uses frequencies (125KHz – 134.2 KHZ).
- High frequency - The frequencies range from 3 to 30 MHz, along with the wavelengths of 10 to 100 meters and reading ranges from 10cm to 1 meter. The acronym HF is used in RFID to represent a tag that uses a high frequency of 13.56MHz to exchange data.
- Ultra high frequency - All the radio-waves from 300 MHz to 3 GHz, with wavelengths ranging from 10 cm to 1 m and measuring distances up to 200 meters. The label using ultra-high frequency is referred to as UHF in RFID. They range from 860MHz – 960MHz.

(Zougar, 2018, para 14)

Origins of RFID Technology

The website Electronic Notes (n.d.) states that (para 1), although RFID originates from the early days of radio, it really took off when radio technology was used to passively identify objects. When Sir Robert Watson-Watt invented radar, he performed the first experiments with radio in this manner. The aircraft (in this case) received a high-powered signal from a single transmitter receiver. (Electronic notes, n.d., para 4)

The radar and IFF systems had demonstrated the concepts of remotely detecting and interrogating objects, but the next stage in RFID history allowed these systems to be used for low-cost commercial applications such as producing electronic surveillance tags for store packaging and these were all forms of passive tags.(Electronic notes, n.d., para 5)

Then, Los Alamos National Laboratories began developing a system to monitor the secure and safe transportation of nuclear materials in the 1970s. A number of readers and transponders were connected to the vehicles transporting the materials as part of the device. These would then be used to identify the truck at different points along its path, therefore, creating an early version of active tags. (Electronic notes, n.d., para 8)

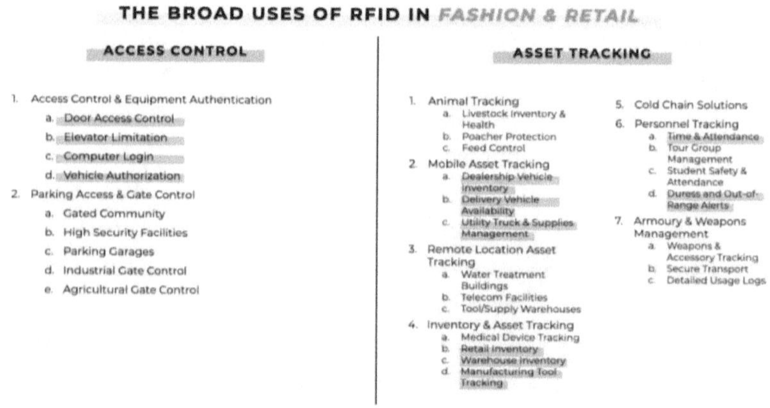

Figure 2: The Broad uses of RFID in The World and in Fashion & Retail

The Broad Uses of RFID Technology in the world, including Fashion & Retail Industry

RFID has a broad range of uses and across all industries too, and the diagram below (Diagram 2) illustrates some of the ways that the world is currently using RFID technology to conduct their business, and the ones highlighted are specifically used in fashion & retail industry. The two umbrella categories are Access Control and Asset Tracking, and they use a mix of active, passive and semi-passive tags, based on the website SkyRFID (2021).

Evolution of RFID technology over the years

The radars were used to send signals and alerts to the planes which were miles away by the Germans, Americans, British and Japanese, during World War II. The transmitters were mounted on the planes to receive signals from the ground radar stations & to send signals back for the identification of the aircraft, leading to the development of the first RFID system by the British, according to American Barcode & RFID, (n.d., para 1).

Since then, RFID technology has progressed significantly RFID tracking technology has progressed to a high level of complexity, offering consumers with unrivalled benefits in a variety of industries, from aircraft to logistics to football. To name a few benefits, RFID leads to improved data quality, faster data gathering, better inventory/asset tracking, and cheaper labour expenses. (American Barcode & RFID, n.d., para 2)

RFID is currently a rapidly expanding sector with a bright future. One aspect fuelling RFID demand is omni-channel retailing. With the advent of eCommerce and mCommerce, improved inventory tracking and management is more crucial than ever, prompting many brands and fashion enterprises to turn to RFID as a solution. (American Barcode & RFID, n.d., para 4)

The demand is so massive that the overall economy is anticipated to reach $24.5 billion by 2020. The forward-thinking businesses are embracing these schemes, the more the demand gets high by the retailers the more the prices would fall. The cost of the tags might collapse up till 5 cents according to EPC Global. Thus, these Radio Frequencies have the potential to generate significant advantage to businesses across a wide range of industries, including Fashion and Retail industry. (American Barcode & RFID, n.d., para 4)

Case Studies in Fashion & Retail with Creative Uses of RFID Technology

1. RFID Wallets.

Turner (2008) describes that skimming with radio frequency identification (RFID) is a type of "digital theft" that allows material from RFID-enabled credit cards to be known and copied. This methodis used to steal a person's identification or credit card information over the internet.(Turner, 2018)

It usually entails scanningthese credit cards (or other devices) remotely to transfer the details on the card. This information can then be copied onto an empty card that would enable it to functionas the original card.(Turner, 2018)

RFID-blocking wallets work by enclosing RFID signals in an electromagnetic enclosure regarded as a Faraday enclosure. This form of technology can make credit cards electromagnetically invisible by dispersing "electrostatic charges or radiation" across the enclosure's perimeter, shielding its matters from electric dispersion.According to Roger A. Grimes, security columnist for InfoWorld, RFID functionality is found on less than 1% of all credit cards in circulation. (Turner, 2018)

If a credit card can be held up to a payment terminal and if one can pay for something without inserting or swiping it across the machine, then it's an RFID-enabled credit card. There are cards that might have been branded as such as well like PayPass or Express Pay, and they have an RFID/contactless payment logo embedded onto them.(Turner, 2018)

The small metallic rectangularchip on the new credit card is actually a microchip that enables more safe purchases, and those are not equivalent to RFID technology. Furthermore, most "contactless payment cards are protected by EMV (chip-and-PIN)."What they essentially do is create a single, encrypted code for every monetary transaction which makes the chip a secure means of communication for the RFID technology. (Turner, 2018)

2. Tommy Hilfiger's Jeans Xplore

Perez (2018) stated that the fashion brand, Tommy Hilfiger, isn't afraid to try out new concepts and technologies. A while ago, Tommy Hilfiger publicized the unveiling of Tommy Jeans Xplore, aninnovativecollection of men's and women's apparel that includes smart-chip embedded technology. Hilfiger's "smart clothing's" objectiveis to incentiviseconsumers for wearing Hilfiger clothing by awarding them points.(Perez, 2018)

The product line comprises of"t-shirts, sweatshirts, hoodies, jeans, jackets, caps, and bags which pair with the Tommy Jeans XploreiOS app over Bluetooth."Consumers can participate in challenges in the app to gain points once they have been paired with their apparel. Users can earn points and receive exclusive incentives from the company when they wear Tommy Hilfiger apparel using Xplore. Through the brand collaboration with Live Nation, loyalty points can be converted into product purchases or tickets to concerts."Gift cards, signed goods, and items from the Tommy Hilfiger archives" are among the prizes that can then be earned with the points that consumers gain. (Perez, 2018)

Tommy Hilfiger said in the official announcement that their intention and motivation is to build a "micro-community of brand ambassadors" who re-use their Tommy Hilfiger products, inadvertently promoting the brand as well. What we can also observe from this strategy, that it's, in a way, reducing rampant consumption of new products too.(Rooney, 2018) Hyper consumerism is a phenomenon driven by fast-fashion and fast-food, and this is occurring in time when the world in experiencing global climate crisis. (Kozlowski, 2019)

3. Salvatore Ferragamo and Moncler

In 2017, Ryan for Launch Metrics (2017) stated that (para 5)Salvatore Ferragamo's quest to eradicate fakes recently prompted the organization to look for ways to ensure product authenticity, which is where RFID technology comes in. Since 2014, they've been embedding microchips in their items, which enable them to not only scan for authenticity but also trace them. This is an excellent usage method for luxury brands, which often bank on their authenticity as well as exclusivity. Similarly, the vintage luxury resale industry can also benefit from RFID tagged products, since they will also be able to authenticate luxury goods. (Rosanna Ryan, 2017, para 5)

Moncler has started to use the RFID technology with the same goal in mind, by providing customers with an app or web service that allows them to scan products they've recently purchased. All of their products can now be scanned on their mobile phone, which is enabled by RFID tag detection, and users can track them as and when needed.(Rosanna Ryan, 2017, para 5).

4. Adidas

Before the coronavirus spread across the world, the sneaker resale market was booming. During the global pandemic, however, the resale market exploded when stay-at-home consumers tallied up their possessions and began selling them. Concerns about brand-name products' authenticity arose as a result, according toKaplan (2021).

One of the reasons why Adidas joined "Avery Dennison's new atma.io platform, which can verify provenance using RFID and other sensors," was to ensure product validity. (Kaplan, 2021)

The brand uses the site for its Infinite Play service, which allows customers to return branded products for Adidas store credit and this was first piloted in the United Kingdom. The items are either resold or recycled by Adidas. As a significant portion of its circularity programme along with strategies to develop the direct-to-consumer market, the company announced that Infinite Play would be launched in the United States later in 2021.(Kaplan, 2021)

By 2025, DTC is expected to account for half of the total revenue, and thereby, potentially doubling Adidas' current e-commerce sector. A major part of the initiative is digital transformation and an omni-channel approach, which includes using RFID technology to handle inventory. (Kaplan, 2021)

5. Zara

Due to the Covid-19 global pandemic, fashion and textile industry was hit just as bad as any other industry since sales almost abruptly stopped, according to Mellor(2021). This led to a lot of brands left with a pile of deadstock due to lack of consumerism. "Closed doors, cancelled orders, missed seasons, changes in consumer preferences. There has been this huge volume of deadstock, more now than ever, all over the world," Stephanie Benedetto, founder of deadstock marketplace Queen of Raw, told Fortune. Before the pandemic affected the businesses around the world, brands would sell their products at discounted rates. Benedetto, like many other brand owners, is looking for ways to minimize waste in the fashion business model. (Mellor 2021)

Looking for more positive outcomes, brands are now trying to find solutions to shift their business models in order to reduce overstocking problem in the first place. Inditex, Zara's parent company, has invested $2.7 billion during the pandemic in the technological amalgamation of its stores, by "tagging every article of clothing with a radio frequency identification (RFID) chip to have mass data of their clothes to streamline demand and supply." (Mellor, 2021)

6. LVMH, Richemont and Prada

Louis Vuitton Moet Hennessey (LVMH) made headlines in May 2019 when it revealed that it was working on a major blockchain project, stated The Fashion Law (2021). The luxury goods conglomerate run by Bernard Arnault hinted the introduction of Aura, a platform that would "serve the entire luxury industry with powerful product tracking and tracing services, built on Ethereumblockchain technology and using Microsoft's [cloud computing service] Azure," through a collaboration with blockchain company ConsenSys and Microsoft.(The Fashion Law, 2021).

Since LVMH's disclosure two years ago, the French group's star brand Louis Vuitton has been occupied with connecting many "new products to blockchain-hosted digital certificates of authenticity" which would exist along with tangible merchandises and provide customers with visibility into the products' provenance. (The Fashion Law, 2021).

Prada will also be using LVMH's technology, according to Lorenzo Bertelli, who is the current head of "marketing and corporate social responsibility at Prada Group," who informed WWD in April 2021, that Prada has "been readying for the Aura blockchain by embedding radio-frequency identification – or RFID – chips into'millions' of items, which began hitting stores in the second half of 2020."(The Fashion Law, 2021)

RFID Technology in the Pandemic and Its Future

As e-commerce expanded during the pandemic, supply chain traceability became more essential. According to "Gayle Meyer, vice president of global marketing and communications at Impinj,"a company that manufactures the silicon-made chips in finalised RFID tags, many firms have started to invest in more savvy technology for their supply chain. "'COVID has made the pain points that existed before [the pandemic] more painful. There have always been supply chain disruptions, but not necessarily at the same scale," she said.'(Kaplan, 2021)

"The increased RFID adoption momentum is due to migrations to e-commerce. RFID drives labour efficiency and improves product availability, he said, as it is easier for employees to know what products are on hand without having to manually search." (Kaplan, 2021)

The existing RFID trade is valued at $500 million plus annually, but the worldwide RFID marketplace is worth approximately $10.7 billion as of 2021, according to Research and Markets, and this value is predicted to increase up to $17.4 billion in 2026. (Kaplan, 2021)

The world could possible need more RFID setups in industrialization to enhanceefficiency, which is a direct consequence of the Covid-19 virus, therefore even healthcare sector may utilise this method to thwart the worldwide Covid-19 blowout. Industries are aware of increasing cost-effectiveness of RFID technology as well as the high returns on investments it brings, making the future of RFID technology, anything but bleak. (Kaplan, 2021)

Conclusions

The Fashion & Retail sector is ranked as the "second highest most polluting industry in the world, second to the Oil Industry" according to Sustain Your Style website (2017). Therefore, sustainability problems are creeping up more widely as stakeholders are gradually becoming more aware of the problems in the industry and how it negatively impacts the consumers' viewpoint about the specific brand, and the industry at large. Therefore to serve their own interests, firms must embrace sustainability or risk alienating customers and investors, and RFID, with its versatile ability to track, trace and account for any and all product types, will be walking hand-in-hand with sustainability, towards a more circular future.(Mellor, 2021)

Due to some of its peculiarities, Trace-ID (n.d.) states that RFID technology has been questioned and transmutedvia its usage in the fashion industry. However, since the introduction of RFID systems, even the most traditional apparelshopsimproved their operations, resulting in the creation of a new business model. As a result, it is important to pay more attention to the fashion benefits of RFID technology. (Trace-ID, n.d.)

References

1. Kaplan, D., 2021. RFID's e-commerce growth spurt.*Supply Chain Dive.* Retrieved from https://www.supplychaindive.com/news/rfid-e-commerce-growth-apparel-stock-fulfillment/599284/

2. Kozlowski, A., 2019. In era of hyper-consumption and in midst of climate change crisis, fast fashion must address its failings. *Firstpost.* Retrieved from https://www.firstpost.com/living/in-era-of-hyper-consumption-and-in-midst-of-climate-change-crisis-fast-fashion-must-address-its-failings-7113391.html

3. Mellor, S., 2021. Fashion retailers are changing how they deal with unsold clothes. *Fortune.* Retrieved from https://fortune.com/2021/04/29/retail-deadstock-unsold-clothes-fashion-supply-chain-covid/

4. Electronic notes (n.d.). *RFID History: Development Timeline » Electronics Notes.* Retrieved 15 May 2021 from https://www.electronics-notes.com/articles/connectivity/rfid-radio-frequency-identification/development-history.php

5. Perez, S., 2018. Tommy Hilfiger has launched a ridiculous line of smart clothing that rewards you for wearing it. *Techcrunch.com.* Retrieved from https://techcrunch.com/2018/07/25/tommy-hilfiger-has-launched-a-ridiculous-line-of-smart-clothing-that-rewards-you-for-wearing-it/

6. American Barcode & RFID, (n.d.).Evolution of RFID.*American Barcode & RFID.* Retrieved 15 May 2021 from https://www.abr.com/evolution-of-rfid/

7. Rooney, V., 2018. Tommy Hilfiger embeds smart chips in new fashion line. *Fox Business.* Retrieved from https://www.foxbusiness.com/retail/hilfiger-embeds-smart-chips-in-new-fashion-line

8. Rosanna Ryan.(2017, October 4). RFID Technology: 5 Ways Fashion Brands Are Using It [blog post]. Retrieved from https://www.launchmetrics.com/resources/blog/rfid-technology-5-ways-fashion-brands-are-using-it

9. Skyrfid.com (n.d.) *RFID Solutions - RFID uses - RFID applications.* Retrieved 15 May 2021 from https://skyrfid.com/RFID_Solutions.php

10. SustainYourStyle (n.d.).*Environmental Impacts of the Fashion Industry.* Retrieved 15 May 2021 from https://www.sustainyourstyle.org/old-environmental-impacts

11. The Fashion Law.(2021). *LVMH, Richemont and Prada Team Up for New Blockchain Venture Aimed at Tracing, Authenticating Luxury Goods.*Retrieved from https://www.thefashionlaw.com/lvmh-richemont-and-prada-team-up-for-new-blockchain-venture-aimed-at-tracing-authenticating-luxury-goods/

12. Trace-ID (n.d.).*Benefits of RFID for the fashion retailing industry.* Retrieved 15 May 2021 from https://www.trace-id.com/benefits-of-rfid-for-the-fashion-and-accessories-retailing-industry/

13. Turner, B., (2018, October 25). RFID Blocking Wallets: Are They Necessary? *Loss Prevention Media.*Retrieved from https://losspreventionmedia.com/

14. Zougar, Y., (2018, August 27). An Introduction to RFID.*Infosec Resources.* Retrievedfrom https://resources.infosecinstitute.com/

XII

Impact of Covid 19 on Employment

Anukriti[1] and Neetu Singh[2]
[1]Research Scholar and [2]Associate Professor
Department of Human Development and Family Studies
Babasaheb Bhimrao Ambedkar University A Central University,
Lucknow
Email Id: anukritibbau03@gmail.com

Abstract

The intent of this paper is to highlight the impact of COVID-19 and its ripple effect on the employment sector, along with factors impacting wages due to lockdowns in India. Keeping with pre-analysis strategy, as documented that COVID-19 adversely impacted the jobs, reduced the typical working hours and hence, increased unemployment numbers, particularly among younger and non-white, not married and less-educated employees. **Objectives:** To review COVID-19 developments and its struggle related to unemployment across the country. To identify and list the challenges, opportunities and limitations posed from the nation-wide and partial lockdowns and their effects on people. To identify the impact on the employment sector throughout this pandemic and the lockdowns. **Methodology:** This paper is written by conducting a review of data gathered from varied secondary sources, such as the relevant sources from Internet including articles, reports, surveys and trends on COVID-19, newspaper and thesis. **Conclusion**: Several reviews conclude that employees who can work virtually have the lower possibility to face the unemployment crisis, whereas employees operating in close proximity with their co-workers have more possibility to get impacted. The states that enforced stay-at-home orders, owing to lockdown, would have higher unemployment. Despite the loss of jobs, age-adjusted price of applied math life suggests that lockdown, as a solution, is more effective in terms of cost.

Keywords: COVID-19, state, wages, jobs, remote work, economy, essential employees, lockdown, unemployment, economic package

Introduction

The unemployment crisis

Like other countries, the Indian economy had to face its own challenges from the pandemic and it did. Due to lockdown, several sectors had a hard stop of production units, goods and raw materials could not have been transported. As a result, the immediate impact was observed on unemployment figures as the industries started reducing the operational cost by cutting down on the number of employees, and hence a considerable job loss happened. A survey conducted in the National capital showed that over 17 percent of unemployment rise was noticed and out of that over 83 percent of women opted out to permanently stop working in the past eight months. Not only in Delhi, but the unemployment percentage also showed an incline move in almost all parts of the country. The data for women's unemployment is also concerning, as their employment growth rate was otherwise also low. Another concerning factor put forward by the Centre for Monitoring Indian Economy (CMIE) in their survey conducted between 2016 and 2020, the female labor data showed a decline from 16.4 percent to 11 percent, which may fall flat of another low of 9 percent owing to the pandemic.

Objectives

- To review COVID-19 developments and its struggle related to unemployment across the country.
- To identify and list the challenges, opportunities and limitations posed from the nation-wide and partial lockdowns and their effects on people.
- To identify the impact on the employment sector throughout this pandemic and the lockdowns.

CMIE analysis also points out the fact that out of the entire workforce of 2019-20, female workers are just above 10 percent. However, if this data is compared to the job loss percentage in just one month (April 2020), unfortunately nearly 14 percent (1.4 in 10) of those who lost their jobs were female employees. The data also reveals an alarming fact that from April to November, while most men were able to recover their jobs, women didn't have identical fate and they just couldn't get the jobs back.

In an interview with Financial Express, Dr KR Shyam Sundar (Human Resource Management professor at Jamshedpur-based XLRI) shared his insight on the country's unemployment-related trends and discussed the volatility in the data as impacted by COVID 19 and its implications to the overall sentiment of the job market. The data trends show that in August last year, the rate of unemployment was nearly over 8 percent, while within next thirty days it dropped to 7 percent and by the end of the year in December, the unemployment data again shoot up to 9 percent.

This uncertainty, with COVID 19, did play its role in the job market along and did raise fears and confusions of what's next and whether to return to job markets or not.

Psychological impact and social impact of quarantine

The reason that these are unprecedented times, uncertainty will be there in the labor market and thus rate of unemployment will also be volatile for some more time. Times like this not only disrupt the earnings of employees which might have resulted in two effects, dis-savings (exhaustion of the money reserves and might also be the pawning of small possessions) and resort to contemporary borrowing that may be weaker and thereby they will find themselves paying inflated interest rates.

It was around this time of the last year, when not only India but the whole world was adjusting and adapting to the new normal. This also impacted the way we work and it has changed forever, along with the way how new hirings are being done. Hiring, done remotely or otherwise, is surging and appears to be on an incline for the coming year too. As far as organizations' acceptance to remote operations are concerned, trends show there is a much-needed trust established already and, for that reason lots of organizations are currently investing in a hybrid model to balance the work life balance providing the greater flexibility. We will still see an incline of positive figures within the economy across various sectors.

Organizations are going to be interested to maneuver aloof from inheritance models and will build their workforce based on performance. Now, workplaces are going to be more flexible, inclusive and soon pushing towards gender equality in their workforce stats. The need for companies and employers to invest in the real-estate will be reassessed and discussed. Having adjusted to virtual workplaces and with growing digital connectivity, there will be a shift from the way we worked. Those organizations and employees who adapted to this shift will be taking advantage of opportunities and growth.

Mr. Srividya Kannan who is a Founder and Director of Avaali Solutions discussed that Hiring has currently improved across sectors throughout the peak of this pandemic. The situation for the section of working personnel from hospitality and tourism who suffered the most impact from the COVID 19 pandemic has also seeming to show positive signs than that of the last year. However, data and trends showed that this pandemic resulted in gender drawback for working class, as more females had to lose their jobs than males. What is more alarming is the fact that females were slow at regaining their jobs back, and this has resulted in clear indication of the gender inequality across sectors. Also, there is a considerable part of country's working class belongs to informal sectors and those suffered job losses too. The lower strata of society and daily wage employees suffered the most because of social distancing also because of the reduced income that fell 46%.

Digital and technical skills are in most demand since the beginning of recovery. There's vital acceleration in adoption of digital technologies not just for margin enhancements however conjointly for client reach via on-line channels".

"The unemployment rate of India's is 24.1% even when the literacy rate is 77% - We can certainly blame the year 2020 with pandemic unfolding in all unexpected ways. Though the numbers aren't looking good, we can't ignore the creative thinking and therefore the numerous fields the year delivered to the forefront. The past few years sure pushed the mechanism of virtual working, permitting folks people all geographies to leap into the race and compete with the established players. Jobs within the technical side of the world like robotics, computing and artificial intelligence as well as the healthcare, Digital advertisement, marketing and Alternate Energy Sources will shortly occupy the highest stack of the opportunities available to us because of the transformation these fields are bringing to the work set up and concept. A big change was also witnessed throughout these times and that is the upliftment of females and their participation within the workforce as key contributors. They have entered the scenario and are here to mark their permanent presence, " as told by Abhinaya, who is heading HR department at Keka, a human resource management solutions company.

Methodology

This paper is written by conducting a review of data gathered from varied secondary sources, such as Internet, articles on COVID-19, newspaper and thesis.

Government actions and suggestions

We can also take a look at the Indian Government actions and timeline to understand this better and have a larger picture -

Based on the poll by Edelman Trust Barometer, 67% people agreed that Government should prioritize saving as many lives possible which means economy isn't the first priority and it will recover slowly. India specific poll showed that 64% people agreed to save lives and 36% agreed to save the jobs. The Government first announced that life will be prioritized but later decided to give an equal importance to both life and the livelihood. By the month of May, the central Government was looking forward to bring the economic activities back on their track where-as some of the Chief Ministers had mixed reactions to that decision considering the evolving circumstances. Indian Prime Minister Modi announced a complete lockdown of 21 days starting from 24 March 2020 mentioning "Only if there is life there will be livelihood". However, in the meeting held between PM and Chief Ministers on 11 April 2020, the PM mentioned "Both, lives and livelihood matter equally". Again, on 14 April 2020, PM announced an extension in the lockdown till 3 May 2020. On 11 May 20202, PM mentioned that the country and its people should prepare itself for this post-pandemic challenges and its effects. It was on 12 May 2020, that PM mentioned how COVID 19, as a pandemic, pushed the need for India to be self-reliant (Atma Nirbhar) and announced Atman Nirbhar Bharat Abhiyan (Self-Reliant Mission for India) economic package.

Timeline

- PM announced an Economic Response Task Force on 19 March 2020. Finance Minister, Nirmala Sitharaman, lead this initiative. RBI was also involved by the Ministry of Finance to monitor the impact on economy on the COVID 19 situation.
- An incentive worth INR 40,995 crore for companies that manufacture electronic goods.
- The UP Government, on 21 March 2020, also made a decision to transfer INR 1,000 to bank accounts of state's daily-wage laborers and soon after some of the other states followed.
- On 24 March 2020, the Prime Minister announced an economic package (INR 15,000 crore) for country's healthcare.
- The finance minister, on 24 March 2020 itself, announced an extension of the dates to file the GST and IT returns. In addition, there was another announcement regarding customs clearances and compliance matters under the Customs Act and associated laws and they were extended to June 2020.

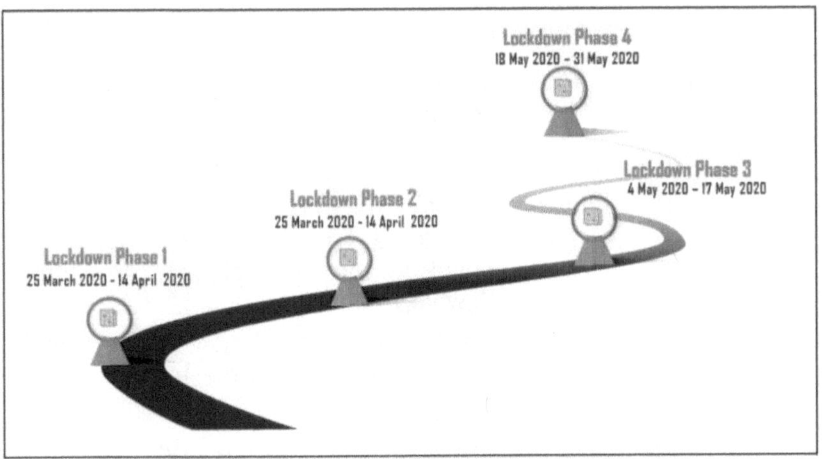

The high-level timeline of the government actions and suggestions

Date	Development
25 March 2020	Central Government came up with the biggest food security scheme on this day.
26 March 2020	Finance Minister, Nirmala Sitharaman, announced an economic relief on this day. o Free LPG cylinders (for about three months) to be provided to the beneficiaries of Pradhan Mantri Ujjwala Yojana o Under the Pradhan Mantri Kisan Samman Nidhi (PM-KISAN), beneficiaries were to be provided their first installment of INR 2000 in April o Both employer and employee contribution of EPF for people earning less than or upto ₹15,000 a month to be borne by Govt. o The same day, India also marked its presence in 'Extraordinary G20 Leaders' Summit held virtually.
27 March 2020	A leeway for three months to hold EMIs was announce by the RBI Governor.
28 March 2020	PM CARES Fund was founded by Prime Minister Modi.
2 April 2020	A loan amounting to 1 billion U.S Dollars was approved for the country by the World Bank.
3 April 2020	Monetary help of INR 17,287 crore was sanctioned to states.
6 April 2020	Announcement on salary cut of leaders, including PM, President and Vice President was made
14 April 2020	An announcement for lockdown extension and its importance was made by the PM

Lockdown Phase 1 (25 March 2020 - 14 April 2020)

Date	Development
15 April 2020	Agriculture and horticulture activities were allowed. IT companies could also start operations with half the staff.
18 April 2020	Change in the FDI policy was announced to safeguard country's companies from international acquisition
21 April 2020	Announcement made about the efforts to revive economic activities
25 April 2020	Relaxations for shops to run was provided, other than liquor shops
28 April 2020	Asian Development Bank approved loan to help deal with pandemic
04 May 2020	Zonal lockdowns, as part of third phase, were announced

Lockdown Phase 2 (15 April 2020 - 3 May 2020)

Date	Development
5-May-2020	A largest cut in development-related expenditure (67 percent), by Maharashtra Government was announced
11-May-2020	India requested Japan for its co-operation in resumption of its companies' (situated in India) activities
12-May to 17-May 2020	An economic package amounting to INR twenty lack crores was announced by the PM. The details of which were shared by the finance minister in the following sessions.
17-May-2020	PM set up a meeting with CMs directed to create plans for resuming economic activities

Lockdown Phase 3 (4 May 2020 - 17 May 2020)

Date	Development
20-May-2020	Further proposal for MSMEs on the economic packages were cleared and announced
25-May-2020	Clearance provided to domestic airline services to resume its services
30-May-2020	Guidance on future Unlocking and or new lockdowns, as applicable, were announced

Lockdown Phase 4 (18 May 2020 - 31 May 2020)

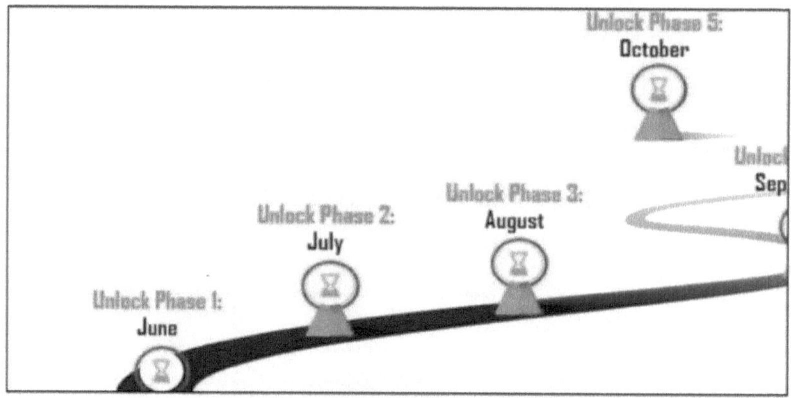

Unlocking in Phased-Manner

Unlock Phase 1 (June):

- The Ministry of home affairs announced the unlock 1 guidelines on 30 May with reopening of markets, malls and shops, religious places in a phased manner.
- Containment zones were to be remained under strict lockdown, which was further to be extended till June 30.

- Salons, Parlors and other shops were allowed to open with timing restrictions.
- Mobile phone manufacturing companies of India were provided with incentives to boost the production of devices production locally.

Unlock Phase 2 (July):

- The Ministry of home affairs announced the unlock 2 guidelines on 29 June with allowing further relaxations but only outside of containment zones.
- Re-starting of schools, colleges, international air travel, metro travel were still not permitted.
- Containment zones were to be remained under strict lockdown, which was further to be extended till June 30.

Unlock Phase 3 (Aug):

- The Ministry of home affairs announced the unlock 3 guidelines on 29 July with allowing further relaxations outside of containment zones.
- Gyms were permitted to re-open, along with yoga centers.
- SOP for the celebration on the Independence Day were defined.
- Containment zones were to be remained under strict lockdown, which was further to be extended till Auf 31.

Unlock Phase 4 (Sep):

- The Ministry of home affairs announced the unlock 4 guidelines on 29 Aug with allowing further relaxations.
- Metro rail travel was permitted in this phase.
- Social gatherings were allowed, however with a maximum limit of 100 people.

Unlock Phase 5 (Oct):

- The Ministry of home affairs announced the unlock 4 guidelines on 30 Sep.
- Permitted activities this time included re-opening of cinema halls with a capping of maximum 50 percent people allowed.
- The states were given the charge to allow schools and colleges to open only after their assessment of the situation.
- Public parks and other entertainment places were also allowed to open in this phase.

The Atma Nirbhar Bharat Abhiyan: An overview

To cope up with the situation and its potential dent to the economy and GDP, the PM of India through his speech on May 12, introduced to the country and its people – the need for the mission called ATMA NIRBHAR BHARAT (Self Reliant India). The focal point of the mission was based on five pillars: Economy, Infrastructure, System, Demography and Demand.

The aim of the mission, as described by the PM in his speech, was to revive the economy, promote locally-made goods, stay vocal for local,and boost production of local goods and make them global to be a self-reliant country. Under this reform, a special economic stimulus was announced by the PM. This amounted to be INR 20 lack crore the 10 percent of the country's GDP. A two-phase campaign was announced to initiate the mission. With Phase 1, Government-led initiatives were explained to support sectors and business financially. Another economic stimulus of INR 2.65 lakh crores was added as part of running this campaign.

Economic situation

Due to COVID-19 pandemic and its uncertainties in the Global Markets, there has to be a downstream impact on the economic situation. Several businesses were either completely or partially shut down, which in turn affected the unemployment rate immediately. Of those, most impacted were sectors that are dependent of movement of people, such as hospitality and tourism. These sectors experienced major layoffs, of those who were not laid-off, there was a significant drop in the income levels. Blue-collar worker considered leaving to their native towns in the uncertainties around.

Stock Markets had a steep fall on the 23 March 2020; SENSEX fell about 4000 points and NIFTY around 1150 points. Manufacturing Industries had to hard stop the goods production due to multiple reasons, there were only a few industries that were allowed to be operational within lockdown guidelines. Demand for fuel reduced in the period, whereas there was a considerable rise in LPG prices. Both import and export of goods fell flat nearly over 47 percent and 36 percent. The earlier predicted GDP of the country for the year was revised from 5.3 percent to 2.5 percent.

The supply chain was disrupted due to lockdowns and, thus, there was a price hike foreseen for essential commodities. This led suppliers to stock the goods and sell it on increased prices. Online deliveries too hampered. Amazon and other platforms could only deliver essential items. The states faced loses in revenue collections.

Unlocking, lockdown relaxions, economic stimulus from the Government served as a major push to the economy in a positive direction. Stock markets started to sense the ease and achieved all time high figures by the end of the year 2020. Several economy indicators started to show green signals, signaling a V shape recovery to the country's economy. The employment data showed positive signs too, however did not reach the old levels.

Side effects of lockdown amidst the pandemic

Whenever there is a pandemic, like COVID 19 today or even any historical pandemic which spreads from human to human, physical is not the only concern. Being quarantined at home triggers another great and more concerning challenge and that is – the impact on mental health and overall well-being.

The psychological impact of the pandemic not only restricts itself to those infected with virus (as they have to be isolated for a considerable period of time), it also takes a great toll on one's family members and friends.

Even those who have not been infected easily fall emotionally sick to the situation, with thoughts like: 'when will we have our old normal days back?' and 'Will it ever be over?'.

These side effects of COVID 19 lockdown are definitely much more severe and may cause drastic consequences (Weir, 2020) and that could be one of reasons of increased case of suicides (Kawohl and Nordt, 2020) over the past few months. Mainly those who live in the areas that have been most affected by the pandemic tend to show unusual behavior associated with anger owing to the struggles of living in a pandemic (Miles, 2014; Suicide Awareness Voices of Education, 2020; Mamun and Griffiths, 2020.).

Several surveys on mental health, during these pandemic times, show that young adults as well as children been struggling with anxiety issues or showing such early symptoms. Those struggling with emotional stress often report factors like loneliness, boredom, irritation, restlessness, nervousness, uneasiness and lack of concentration and enthusiasm in doing day to day activities.

Adults also often feel overwhelmed with the situation. Compared to the normal days, they have a lot more work to handle, kids are always at home and demand extra time and attention, seeking domestic services help that was earlier an option for few, now is not. Working parents have to multi-task too.

Restriction on outdoor leisure activities that earlier proved to be a stress-buster, for any age, is either risky or not possible. Another section of population notably suffering from stress is the HealthCare Workers (HCWs). They have been under both physical as well as emotional stress since the start of the pandemic. They are over-worked and exhausted and have to face traumatic situation day and night. There has been immense pressure on health-care personnel and they have been fighting hard for more than a year and saved countless lives putting themselves at risk. As a matter of fact, HCWs go through greater levels of psychophysical stress (Mohindra et al., 2020). HCWs, by the nature of their job, have to face traumatic conditions, and therefore often are a patient of secondary traumatic stress disorder (Zaffina et al., 2014).

HCWs UN agency who were deployed in COVID-19 duty in second- and third-line wards reported depression, anxiety, sleep-discomfort (Lai et all., 2020). Due to the fact that they are always around the infected people and may infect their loved ones when they go back home after duty, they always have to deal with their neurotic thoughts (Brooks et al., 2020). Upon an evaluation of a survey conducted on HCWs of Italy, it was observed that the mental-state of female HCWs as well as front line people was impacted and they had elevated stress levels. Spoorthy et al. (2020) reviewed the COVID-19 impact on HCWs and observed that about approximately about 60 to 80 percent of HCWs are girls with a mean age group between 24-40 years and have been under depression and distress because of the pandemic.

Liang et al. (2020) additionally devised a correlation between age and depression resulting from the pandemic. While young (less than 30 years old) medical staff had depression owning to the concern of passing the infection to their loved ones in the family. Medical staff above 50+ years old, had a different reason for the depression, that is either patient's death, exhaustive and prolong working hours or not sufficient availability PPE kits.

Cai et al. (2020) additionally investigated that the level of nervousness and anxiety was much more in nurses than doctors. Thus, we can conclude on the basis of these surveys done on young, adults and HCWs (who are greatly exhausted due to the nature of their job) – there is an absolute need to find solutions to take care of mental well-being also, along with physical and financial health. As per Lancet Global Mental Health Commission (Patel, 2018), technology can play its part to monitor and control anxiety and stress levels and upscale self-efficacy (Kang et al., 2020; Xiao et al., 2020).

Opportunity amidst the crisis

No doubt the healthcare system is going through an emergency like situation, but we should also notice that India has been playing a critical role in the field of medicine production and export. India is mass producing the PPE kits, ventilators, surgical masks, medical goggles and turning out to be a big export hub, ranking 3rd in the field of medicine production. The cost of production is also very less compared to the western countries. Last financial year 2020 - 2021, the global medicine market saw a fall of 2%, whereas Indian exports saw an 18% increase amounting to 24.44 billion dollars. India didn't just increase the export to the developing countries but developed countries like the US and other European nations.

India is reaching a new level in the field of vaccine manufacturing to the extent that 60% of the vaccine being used in the world is produced by India. India has provided around 600 million vaccine doses to over 80 nations and is targeting to increase the production further. The Central drug standard control organization has also taken multiple important decisions in this direction.

Foreign companies are looking forward to increase the collaboration with India to mass produce their vaccine, the Russian vaccine Sputnik is one of such collaborations where India will produce 60 to 70 of the global requirements. America, Australia, Japan are also looking forward to produce over 1 bill ion doses by 2022 and India will be playing a bigger role in that too. This would also boost the independent India movement by the central government where the focus would be on producing the expensive medicines in India and take on the work from the companies which moved out of China which could also invite investment of around 500 billion.

Under the PLI scheme, the government has assigned 70 billion rupees to promote the manufacturing of raw materials needed for medicines. This overall will boost the pharmaceutical sector of the country. There is no doubt the COVID-19 has given an opportunity to the country for medical research and development. Considering the current circumstances, India will now focus on mass producing the Covid-19 vaccine and getting the citizens vaccinated.

On the World map, India is emerging as a hub of global pharmacy and Corona vaccine. Pharma sectors will keep the push on the research and related expenses to make sure India is more independent and is also not impacted by the current ban by the US on the raw products being used in the vaccine. This would in tum attract the foreign investment and reinforce the internal health infrastructure of the country.

Policies for the recovery

With vaccines not being available or have limited availability and not an effective cure or prevention in place, those countries that plan to re-open their business and related activities countries must find an appropriate and balanced for businesses to operate without risking the surge in infections. At a greater level, organization will have to work hand in hand with Governments to create adequate reforms and policies in favor of workable labor market conditions and can be scaled to broader levels, when applicable.

Precise actions are needed to be implemented to handle uneven and the uncertain cause of the catastrophe in order for settling the issues faced by the lower working-class. The G20 policy makers in this sense, might want to consider the following policy guidelines, based on their country's circumstances:

1. Following appropriate safety measure: Resolving the health-related crisis, undoubtedly, is a vital requirement to tackle any other form of crisis, say job loss or dent on the economy. As the countries reopen, it becomes significant to introduce directives and strategies to make sure that a workplace upholds to proper safety measures. In the similar context the small and med-sized entities would require extra support to practices supporting workplace health and safety. Exclusive benefits related to the illness and paid leave to take care of the family, including a leave for parenting (or a parental leave), as applicable, must be formalized and also be applied to all types of working section to promote well-being of people. Re-connecting employees on sick leave with professional reintegration will also promote the trust.

2. Establishing schemes that promote job retention: Job retention arrangements may need to be improved as few sectors will have to be opened soon, however few others would not be able to resume the normal activities. Possible actions to advance cost-effectiveness and sustainability include: demanding companies to accept costs in partial arrangements; ensuring the support is time-bound and able to adapt to the evolving conditions and also promoting the movement of employees from subsidized to unsubsidized jobs, by delivering relevant trainings during the reduced working hours.

3. Making sure the required protection to the income and still proving the assistance in searching the jobs. The financial pressure will continue to mount but the government needs to make sure that those who are in urgent need do get the required support. As the nations would recover along with their economies, we need to have a good balance between maintaining good support and promoting new job searches. These supporting steps and other measures must be followed to support the jobseekers. Also, training and relevant support through the various readiness programs may assist jobseekers.

4. Promoting job creation: With small and big economic reforms, there should be provision for the hiring subsidies and incentives, offering bonus to the employees to boost job creations.

Rebuilding the labor market

The pandemic has proven to be a tough crisis for labors, daily-wage workers, small businesses, fixed-term employees and especially for all those sectors where remotely working is not possible.

The responsible leaders have to soon begin working towards the recovery process in order to make the way forward and open new avenues for the worst-hit workers. There is a crucial need to make reforms that offer a practical and fair approach to safeguard jobs from any future crisis like these.

With a motive to Building Back Economy Better, policy makers need to offer a prudent solution to support those with impacted work as well as incomes especially the underprivileged and vulnerable sections of the society to avoid future disparity and inequality.

The policies underlining this approach might need to be devised in a manner that it could be implemented easily at the any level, say country, a state, or a sector. This can later be replicated within specific settings in ways that it can be helpful for people expected to be benefiting from the same. Several measures can be implemented for the same:

1. Facilitate job retention policies or schemes that can handle the economic uncertainties due to pandemic or such emergency economic crisis. Also, adoption of such campaigns that can ensure that there is adequate financial support being provided to the worst-hit employees.
2. Supporting the workforce with actionable reforms, such as revisiting the old or existing policies and frameworks to ensure that people at work receive equal treatment irrespective of their job profile or position.
3. Adding versatility to employment services and updating the work conditions. Proposing and implementing reforms with strong institutional capability while maintaining the quality of the services. This means ramping up the policy infrastructure in such a way that if any uncertainty like this arises, it can be dealt without a dent on operations.
4. Proposing such reforms and policies to broader levels, such as for the entire sector. There is a need for responses so that policy makers can go ahead and make the changes while also devising workable recovery strategies.

5. Making necessary changes in fully operation and existing employment framework so that the unprecedented risks can be mitigated.
6. Adding a combination of reforms and campaigns that facilitates a seamless transition to the formal economy from the informal one.
7. Implementing gender equality policies that could be bolstered in a plethora of areas or sections within the labor market –

- Promoting a family-friendly work environment or arrangements that are suitable for women as well along with flexible leave policies;
- Seamless access to child care services along with complementary services;
- Promotion of entrepreneurship programs solely focused on women and their leadership skills to increase their participation;
- Spread awareness against domestic violence and promote a harassment-free work environment to see enhanced participation from women as well.

8. Offering a provision of skill-development opportunities for workforce.

Conclusions

The detailed analysis reveals the negative impact of the pandemic and accompanying lockdown on the employees from different background and ethnicities between the European and Asian countries, chosen to be part of the survey. The most badly affected being the underprivileged or minorities who are often part of low productivity sectors.

It will be safe to assume that employees are vulnerable to losing their jobs during the pandemic lockdown and have been faced with a wave of uncertainty persisting in the job sector, according to our analysis. Workers in the said category have most been impacted negatively in financial terms due to the confinement measures as they had negligible income, as a result.

For the fiscal year 2020-2021 of the Indian economy, we may continue to see the impacts of lockdown and persistent economic crisis. As of current month, i.e. May 2021, while writing this, there the same lockdown measures in place. While there still is a lot of uncertainty, one can hope with the positive point of view that the initiation of recovery will take place in a phased manner, gradually though. The road to recovery might hit some bumps due to implications and concerns surrounding the control of the subsequent spread of COVID 19.

Also, the future recovery process seems vague at the moment and will largely rely upon the mode of economic recovery chosen by the country. There is a possibility of three different modes of recovery – V shape (optimistic), U Shape (moderate recovery with time) and W shape (feeble).

One can assume the possibility of implementation of all three given the current scenario. There are, however, some positive sides to this for a powerful recovery. One of the things that work to our advantage is that the Indian economy is least affected by the prevalent worldwide financial conditions.

There is also the need for strong and sturdy reforms and polices so that the nation can rise again from crisis such as these. It is great that states have been working together as a unit like never before amidst the crisis and this will pave the road to recovery but it is hard to tell how much time will this take.

It is also crucial that the government adopt an agile financial approach, something like a two-pronged approach, to pave way for the fast and powerful rebound. This calls for contributions from large institutions and sectors, especially banking sector and other financial establishments as well as agencies to design and implement policies and put them into action as per the demand.

Next, it is most significant to involve and encourage big and medium enterprises to be adding their contributions in lifting the situation. The road to recovery is going to be huge task that will need multiple tasks and phases. Not alone Government, the situation will also require support from various non-government organisations, privatesector, industrialists, their staff as well as the general public. There is a need to inculcate responsibility amongst every citizen to be equally responsible and supportive for the huge task of the road to economic recovery, let alone the government.

References

1. Andersen, A. L., Hansen, E. T., Johannesen, N., & Sheridan, A. (2020). Pandemic, shutdown and consumer spending: lessons from scandinavian policy responses to COVID-19. Papers arXiv, May 2005.
2. Alvarez, F., Argente, D., and Lippi, F. (2020). A simple planning problem for Covid-19 lockdown. Covid Econ. 14, 1–33. doi: 10.3386/w26981

3. Barbisch, D., Koenig, K., and Shih, F. (2015). Is there a case for quarantine? Perspectives from SARS to Ebola. Dis. Med. Pub. Health Prepar. 9, 547–553. doi: 10.1017/dmp.2015.38

4. Brooks, S., Webster, R. S., Woodland, L., Wessely, S., Greenberg, N., et al. (2020). The psychological impact of quarantine and how to reduce it: rapid review of the evidence. Lancet 395:10227. doi: 10.1016/S0140-6736(20)30460-8

5. Cao, W., Fang, Z., Hou, G., Han, M., Xu, X., Dong, J., et al. (2020). The psychological impact of the COVID-19 epidemic on college students in China. Psych. Res. 287:112934. doi: 10.1016/j.psychres.2020.112934

6. Day, T., Park, A., Madras, N., Gumel, A., and Wu, J. (2006). When Is Quarantine a Useful Control Strategy for Emerging Infectious Diseases? Am. J. Epidemiol. 163, 479–485. doi: 10.1093/aje/kwj056

7. del Rio-Chanona, R. M., Mealy, P., Pichler, A., Lafond, F., & Farmer, J. D. (2020). Supply and demand shocks in the COVID-19 pandemic: An industry and occupation perspective. Covid Economics, Centre for Economic Policy Research., 6, 65–103.

8. Fana, M., Tolan, S., Torrejón Pérez, S., Urzi Brancati, M. C., & Fernández-Macías, E. (2020). The COVID confinement measures and EU labour markets. Luxembourg: Publications Office of the European Union.

9. Fessell, D., and Goleman, D. (2020). How Healthcare Personnel Can Take Care of Themselves. US: HBR.

10. Li, L. Z., and Wang, S. (2020). Prevalence and predictors of general psychiatric disorders and loneliness during COVID-19 in the United Kingdom. Psych. Res. 291, 0165–1781. doi: 10.1016/j.psychres.2020.113267

11. Garcia-Castrillo, L., Petrino, R., and Leach, R. (2020). European Society For Emergency Medicine position paper on emergency medical systems' response to COVID-19. Eur. J. Emerg. Med. 27, 174–1777. doi: 10.1097/mej.0000000000000701

12. Grassi, L., and Magnani, K. (2000). Psychiatric Morbidity and Burnout in the Medical Profession: An Italian Study of General Practitioners and Hospital Physicians. Psychother. Psychosom. 69, 329–334. doi: 10.1159/000012416

13. Kang, L., Ma, S., and Chen, M. (2020). Impact on mental health and perceptions of psychological care among medical and nursing staff in Wuhan during the 2019 novel coronavirus disease outbreak: A cross-sectional study. Brain Behav. Immun. 87, 11–17. doi: 10.1016/j.bbi.2020.03.028

14. Kawohl, W., and Nordt, C. (2020). COVID-19, unemployment, and suicide. Lancet Psych. 7, 389–390. doi: 10.1016/s2215-0366(20)30141-3

15. Mohindra, R. R. R., Suri, V., Bhalla, A., and Singh, S. M. (2020). Issues relevant to mental health promotion in frontline health care providers managing quarantined/isolated COVID19 patients. Asian J. Psych. 51:102084. doi: 10.1016/j.ajp.2020.102084

16. Orgilés, M., Morales, A., Delvecchio, E., Mazzeschi, C., and Espada, J. (2020). Immediate psychological effects of the COVID-19 quarantine in youth from Italy and Spain. PsyArXiv 2020, 1–13. doi: 10.1017/s0033291720001841

17. Patel, V. (2018). The Lancet Commission on global mental health and sustainable development. Lancet 392, 1553–1598. doi: 10.1016/S0140-6736(18)31612-X

18. Roden-Foreman, K., Solis, J., Jones, A., Bennett, M., Roden-Foreman, J., Rainey, E., et al. (2017). Prospective Evaluation of Posttraumatic Stress Disorder and Depression in Orthopaedic Injury Patients With and Without Concomitant Traumatic Brain Injury. J. Orthop. Trauma 31, e275–e280. doi: 10.1097/BOT.0000000000000884

19. Rossi, R., Socci, V., and Pacitti, F. (2020). Mental Health Outcomes Among Frontline and Second-Line Health Care Workers During the Coronavirus Disease 2019 (COVID-19) Pandemic in Italy. JAMA Netw Open. 3:e2010185. doi:

20. Tam, C., Pang, E., Lam, L., and Chiu, H. (2004). Severe acute respiratory syndrome (SARS) in Hong Kong in 2003: stress and psychological impact among frontline healthcare workers. Psychol. Med. 34, 1197–1204. doi: 10.1017/s0033291704002247

21. Weir, K. (2020). Grief and COVID-19: Mourning our bygonelives. Washington: American Psychological Association.

22. Zaffina, S., Camisa, V., Monducci, E., Vinci, M., Vicari, S., and Bergamaschi, A. (2014). Disturbo post traumatico da stress in operatori sanitari coinvolti in un incidente rilevante avvenuto in ambito ospedaliero. La Med. Del Lav. 105:2014.

23. https://www.ilo.org/wcmsp5/groups/public/---dgreports/-cabinet/documents/publication/wcms_756331.pdfcabinet/documents/publication/wcms_756331.pdf

24. https://www.financialexpress.com/jobs/covid-19-impact-coronavirus-led-to-a-volatile-employment-trend-throughout-2020/2224185/

XIII

Severe Effects of the Massive COVID-19 during the Pandemic: Facing the Job Crisis

Reema Ningthoujam[1] and Harish Kumar Dhingra[2]
[1]Research Scholar and [2]Assistant Professor
Mody University of Science and Technology, Rajasthan, Sikar,
Lakshmangarh-332311
Email ID: harishdhingra2000@gmail.com

Abstract

One of the most severe negative impacts of the novel and deadly COVID-19 pandemic is the loss of employment. To prevent spreading of the contagious disease, practices and measures such as social-distancing, self-quarantine, national as well as state-wide lockdown were imposed leading to decreased working hours and thus a hugely significant impact on wages too. However, there are different types of workers based on the fields which they serve among which workers that depend on heavy physical activities affect the most, threatening their survival. As a result, there is a sudden displacement of workers due to which the economic activity came to a halt. To lift the downfall of the economy, restrictions implemented and lockdown is starting to ease across the globe, however, we will come into contact with more people which will increase the chances for the virus to spread even more. Waiting until the corona cases decline for the normal work to be resumed requires keeping a painful lockdown for a longer period. As we travel on this unprecedented journey, adopting new principles such as self-reliance, appropriate use of the internet and technology might elevate the economy in this uncertain environment. This study overviews the impact of the epidemic on employment, gender disparity in the labour market during the crisis, and ways to mitigate the negative implications even in the post Covid-19 world.

Keywords: COVID-19, employment, economy, self-reliance, gender disparity

Introduction

COVID-19, which is also known as the Coronavirus disease or simply COVID, is a highly infectious disease which is caused by SARS-CoV-2 (Severe Acute Respiratory Syndrome Coronavirus 2) where it was first reported in Wuhan, China, in the middle of somewhere December 2019 (Page, Hindshaw & McKay, 2021). Zimmer (2021) explains that ever since the deadly disease has spread throughout every continent except Antarctica leading to and ongoing global pandemic. The transmission mainly occurs when an infected person sneezes, cough, or speak and is in close contact with another person (WHO, 2020; CDC 2021), due to which the governments are now mandating to practice self-isolation and physical distancing in areas affected by the outbreak (Qian & Jiang, 2020). Such an act minimizes close contact between individuals and hence resulted in the slow spread of the virus. Challenges such as quarantines, lockdowns in affected areas, night curfews to avoid unnecessary gatherings, the closing of schools, universities, religious places, work-places, gyms, theatres, or malls, reducing half the number of seats in public transports, etc. were imposed all across the country. Such methods slow down the wild spread of the disease but at the same time, a lot of people are suffering a tremendous and intolerable burden of loss. The sudden emergence of the pandemic is dealing a sharp blow to country economies and labor market crisis. The mandatory lockdown measures adopted have wreaked havoc on global trade and restricted economic activities. Walter (2020) reports that there is also evidence of developing countries facing disorder in trade and supply chains which lead to triggering economic ripple effect.

Implications of the pandemic for Employment across the Globe

ILO Monitor, (2020a) shows that on 18th March 2020, The International Labour Organization (ILO) first survey on COVID-19 had observed a sudden rise in unemployment and underemployment between 5.3 million and 24.7 million from a base level of 188 million in 2019. ILO's 5th Monitor on impact of COVID-19 which was released on 30 June 2020 reports that the labour market recovery during the second half of 2020 will remain uncertain. It was also estimated that the loss of working-hour could range between 140-340 million full-time jobs in the last quarter of the year (ILO Monitor, 2020b). In the ILO's 7th Edition, the global labor income for the year 2020 is estimated to have reduced by approximately 8.3 percent, which equals to US$3.7 trillion, or 4.4 percent of GDP i.e. Global Gross Domestic Product. American workers experienced a massive labour income loss by around 10.3% while the smallest income loss was seen in Asia and the Pacific by 6.6% (ILO Monitor, 2021). In the Least Developed Countries such as Bangladesh, one study reports that as of June, 89.6% of Bangladeshi households have experienced quite a fall in their income as low as 94.8% with no adequate feed stocks, while 34% were reported to no access to clean and hygienic water (World Vision, 2020). In Senegal, a study reports increase in unemployment rate by 0.2% in 2020 and 0.15% in 2021 (UNDP, 2020a). In Yemen too, a study showed that 40% of formal workers have lost their employment and their loss in income has become significant, while 79% revealed a reduced income of at least a fifth (Norwegian Refugee Council, 2020). In Ethiopia also, evidence of drastic income losses due to a fall in employment rates was observed significant, which affects 55% of the households between April and May, 46% in between May-June, and a drastic reduction of 50% in the month of July (Open Knowledge Repository). Uganda, which is also one of the least developed countries experienced the most adverse change of job loss. The negative economic impacts of the pandemic resulting in the closures of business affecting millions of Ugandan workers, these consequences are expected to rise the number of poor people by an additional of 2.6 million (UNDP, 2020b). As compared to other parts of the world, the estimated loss of working hours in low-income countries is much lower. Many workers in low-income countries are daily wage laborers and low-skilled workers. Their nature of work mostly depends on physical activity which is why working from home and teleworking is not an option for them.

Figure 1: Youth Unemployment Rate in G20 Countries (2020)

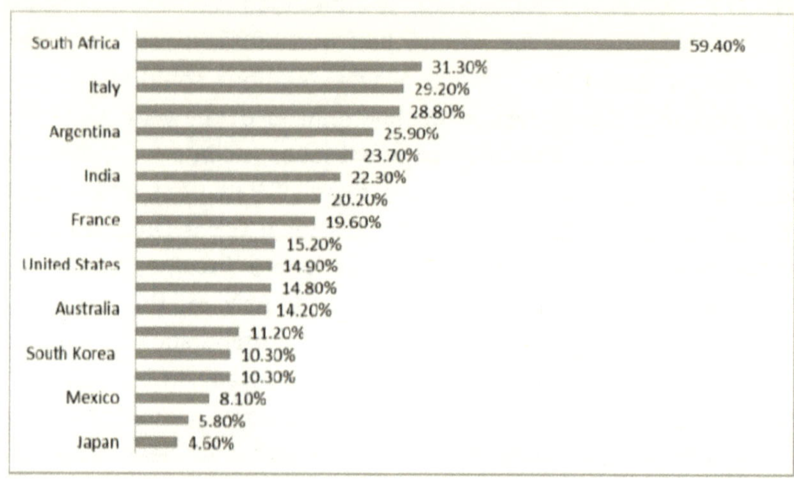

Source:ILOSTAT database

International Labour Organization and Organisation for Economic Co-operation and Development, "Global Skills Trends, Training Needs and Lifelong Learning Strategies for the Future of Work".(June 2018) stated that in all the various G20 countries too, when the pandemic hits, the jobs gap was widening rapidly and thus weak employment growth. Deborah (2020) revealed that in all G20 countries, in 2019, out of 3.8 billion working-age population, around 1.5 billion were out of the labor force, while some 280 million population were underutilized. Also, in the subsequent year, the youth unemployment rate in G20 countries was tremendously high, ranging from 4.6% in Japan to a high 59.4% in South Africa **(Figure 1)** (ILOSTAT database). Only three G20 countries (Japan, Germany, and Mexico) showed single-digit youth unemployment rates.

Gender disparity and the Labour market

Gender gaps in employment even before the onset of the pandemic were still considerable in labor markets. Even after the crisis too, a similar pattern is observed but more employment losses and thus higher unemployment are being experienced by the women as compared to men. According to the Bureau of Labour Statistics May 2020, women's unemployment rate stood at 14.3% while a decrease unemployment rate of 11.9% was observed in men.

Some major causes of the large impact on women's unemployment in the labor market are stated in the following lines.

The first cause relates to the unemployment causes triggered by the lockdown. As per the guidelines issued, social distancing measures and quarantine methods were implemented. Business shutdown which includes service sectors such as salons, restaurants, tourism, hospitality, etc. has been severely affected. These economic sectors are where women represent the majority of the workforce, leading to a high unemployment rate during the Corona crisis. Another cause that leads to employment loss affecting women workers is the disparity between women and men when it comes to fulfilling household responsibilities. When the pandemic hits, schools and day-care centers were shut down and children were sent back to home. Parents having young children are affected the most as there is an increase in the childcare burden. This hugely increased childcare needs during working hours. As compared to men, women are the ones that have taken on a larger share of the extra childcare responsibilities (Alon et al., 2020).

Figure 2: Labour force participation rate between women and men (2020)

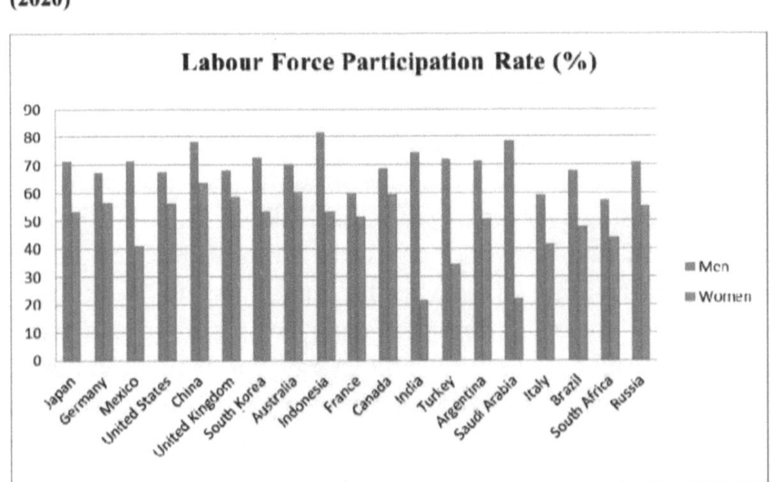

Source: ILOSTAT Database

Women mainly were the ones who were called upon to pick up the household tasks. As a result, school and daycare closures are forcing working mothers to take leave or resign based on their inability to work at regular intervals that conflict with child care duties. Since many schools will remain closed for the said period, women are forcing themselves in the position of home-schooling their children to keep up with their educational studies. This is one of the main reasons why women are unlikely of returning to work. Figure 2 illustrates the comparison of labour force participation rate between men and women (2020) in most of the G20 countries during the crisis. The data showed that the women's labor force participation rate in all the G20 countries was relatively lower than men. The lowest women labor participant rate was observed in India at only 21.5% followed by Saudi Arabia which stands at 21.9%. However, in countries like France, Germany, and Russia, measures have been taken specifically to allow some daycare centres to remain open, with limited staff, ensuringthe child care of essential workers which can be looked after.

Mitigating the unemployment consequences of the crisis

There have been large income loss due to economic shutdown and thus economic revival requires a 'big push'. Restoring such demand is a huge challenge itself and it is difficult to think how it can be revived. Following are the few policies that can be adopted to combat the job crisis due to pandemic:

1. To encourage teleworking from home

Supporting those who can telework from their homes is one key measure that can reduce the exposure of workers to the virus. Although the number of people teleworking either full-time or on a part-time basis has been gradually increasing over the recent years (EUROSTAT, 2018), the pandemic has proven itself that teleworking ensures the continuity of the business. Teleworking offers the advantages for employees to work from their convenient locations away from the employer's premises, can avoid office distractions as well as saves time and energy. But at the same time, there may also be high risks such as detachment from fellow employees, isolation which might, later on, cause psychological disorders. In the meanwhile, teleworking is unusual and is used for a certain period only. In any case, to stop the spread of the contagious disease, workers who are compatible with teleworking should be allowed to work from their home during the crisis including those in temporary employment too (ILO, 2020c).

Unfortunately, not all workers share the same fate. For such workers who are unable to work from home, their respective countries should issue strict health guidelines and implement comprehensive occupational safety and health (OSH) standards. Adopting the use of partitioning walls in the workplace, providing Personal Protective Equipment, such as masks, hand sanitizers, gloves, etc., to restrict the further spread of the virus. This will allow the workers that cannot work from their convenient places to be physically present on their workplace or companies' premises. Also, vulnerable groups of the population include workers that depend on physical proximity, refugee workers, or migrants, where a majority of them are illiterate. For them, it is necessary to provide information on Covid-19 related issues, update existing policies, health, and safety guidelines in a language where they can understand. However, it is more likely that the adoption of telework will remain much higher than they were before the onset of the pandemic.

2. Initiation of paid sick leave policies

Saint et al. (2018) notes that the underlying idea of paid sick leave is to protect (i) the workers' health allowing sick workers to self-isolate and let them recover fully at home. Going to work during this period may lengthen the duration of illness and further reduce productivity; (ii) workers' incomes; (iii) preserving the workers' employment by keeping their relationships intact during a temporary sickness period. Almost all the OECD and G20 countries have started expanding paid sick leave regulations for workers suffering from this illness or in quarantine. Similarly, other countries also started adopting statutory sickness benefits. In countries such as Austria, Germany, Italy, and Switzerland, the sickness pay benefits may last 5-15 days but can be extended up to several weeks or months, and in Netherlands up to two years (OECD, 2020). United Kingdom, Government of 'Coronavirus Support for Employees, Benefit Claimants and Businesses'. (2020, March 16) initiated paid sick leave to all the economy workers which includes casual workers, who are in self isolation. Portugal has also adopted provisions for migrant laborers ensuring national social protection schemes which are provided to them as well and have access to public services. The country has also started taken measures to treat them as permanent residents during the said period(ILO, 2020d). The United States too started introducing a scheme for two weeks of mandatory sick pay for workers suffering from COVID-19 related symptoms. Also, the Federal law in Russia also establishes that the number of temporary disability benefits cannot be lower than the minimum wage for periods of disability from 1st of April to 31st December, 2020.

In some countries, despite the measures taken up, the sickness benefits only cover a small fraction of the previous earnings and the recommended period of self-isolation for those people associated with COVID-19 symptoms is relatively shorter. Individual groups who are associated with non-standard work tend to be excluded from the sickness benefits(OECD, 2019). At times like this, policymakers should establish systems that make paid sick leave systems adaptable to them so that these mechanisms can be readily scaled up during future health crisis, learning job retention schemes from this pandemic experience.

3. To provide income security and job retention schemes to under priviledged or affected worker

There is an urgent need to establish robust job retention schemes such as Short-Term Work (STW) schemes to mitigate the crisis on unemployment. STW schemes are those public programs that allow companies to temporarily lessen the number of working hours and ensure income support for the affected workers so that it can prevent permanent lay-offs and maintain the employment relationship. This scheme offers an opportunity to compensate financial relief for enterprises to compensate the income lost during the pandemic. Muller and Schulten (2020) claimsthat, more than 42 million applications for STW schemes were applied at the end of April 2020, in the EU27. Also job-protection measures like temporary lay-offs, where the worker's employment contract is maintained but need not work at all for a period, yet they receive a certain level of income can be adopted. A common characteristic that both the schemes share is that workers are paid for more labor than they supply. However, there may still be groups of vulnerable workers who will not be benefitted from such schemes. Thus, additional support like supplementary income support may be required for them. Figure 3 shows the comparison between the approved applications and actual participation in the job retention schemes (May 2020).

Social protection schemes can also be provided by extending protection to vulnerable categories which include young unemployed people, below poverty line families, and mostly single parents who are facing problems due to school closures, which can be used to replace income and thus stabilize the economy during the crisis. Regardless of their employment status, the social protection system offers a minimum level of protection to all. However, the situation of perilous workers requires special attention.

Figure 3: Job retention schemes participation across G20 countries

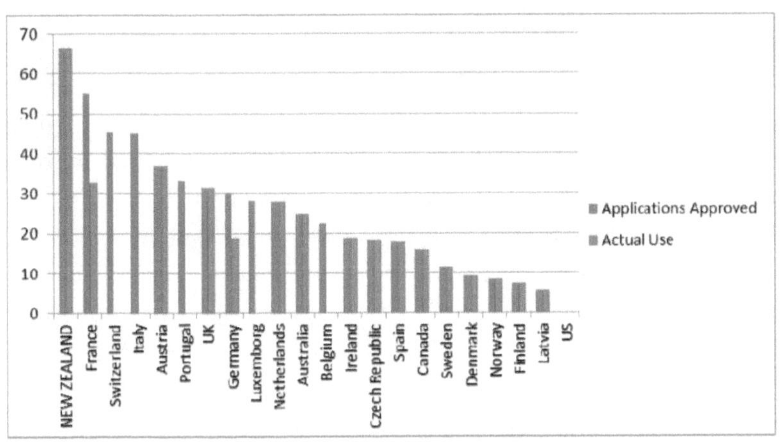

Source: OECD Employment Outlook 2020 (Chapter 1)

4. Designing liquidity support for firms

The lockdown measures have induced many businesses to shut down temporarily that led to the significant liquidity stress on businesses. The sudden fall down on revenues have forced the firms to cut employment and delayed capital spending to avoid bankruptcy.In order to lessen the liquidity shortages, national authorities can adopt a wide range of emergency measures such as supporting firms' liquidity. Several design approaches, including some forms of subsidized term funding, loan guarantees,as well as tax-related credit guarantees are some of the measures that many countries have started to adopt to support companies' financial liquidity. Such support usually targets small and medium-sized enterprises (SMEs) as they are often seen as being at greater risk of financing difficulty (Jeasakul, 2020). Liquidity support schemes can be discussed under two approaches: through lenders and Special Purpose Vehicles (SPVs). Here, in the lenders' scheme, lenders play a major role in providing liquidity support to businesses. By doing so, the lenders' may benefit from term funding provided by central banks or government subsidy on funding costs. Many emerging market economies have started adopting some policies of this approach by setting up financing programs and credit guarantees. Under the schemes that operate via SPVs (Special Purpose Vehicles),the SPVs are created to acquire credit extended by lenders according to the prescribed conditions (Monetary and Capital Markets). Generally, the central banks create and finance these SPVs whose losses are largely backstopped by the governments. Lenders' credit risk is lessen as part of the loans are sold to the SPVs. However, the considerations of liquidity support schemes depends on country circumstances. Drop in sales is observed in every parts of the world and induced a sharp drop in the economy. It is believed that such type of scheme introduction might make the economy return quickly to its pre-pandemic level. It is therefore necessary to provide firms with the liquidity needed in order to avoid bankruptcies on a large scale.

Conclusions

The coronavirus disease continues to spread across the globe and has brought the economy to a halt over the past year. The crisis has revealedthe deep-rooted labor market fragilities and structural inequalities where it is giving a catastrophic effect on working hours as well as earnings too. To tackle some of these crisis responses, teleworking, which can be seen as an advancement to develop new flexible ways of working can be considered but potentially consequences of long-term effects should also be considered at the same time. The lockdown measures implemented trigger changes in direct employment loss to many young people, self-employed workers, ethnic minorities, migrants, non-standard and fixed-term workers. We also observe that women's position in the labour market is likely to be persistent as women are the ones who bear major childcare responsibilities. It is high time to change the social norms towards a more equal childcare obligation between men and women. Such changes might ultimately enhance women's labour force participation rate and no doubt will reduce the gender wage gap. Given the extremity of the ongoing health and economic crisis, more examination on the consequences of the Covid-19 on women's jobs and gender inequality in a vast range of countries is highly needed. Also, initiations taken up in many countries such as sickness benefit schemes, STW schemes, liquidity support schemes, and unemployment benefits have found to be significant to sustain the incomes of many financially vulnerable groups thus minimizing initial job losses. But still, some workers having informal jobs and their families are bound to miss out the opportunities even in countries that have the most advanced social protection. Situations are even worse in countries having large non-standard sectors where many people lose work without any access to income. This fight against the deadly virus is yet to be won, however, now is the right time to stay adapted to this "new normal" and right away starting the tasks of building the unpredictable future way better. The decision that we make today will directly affect the way this pandemic unfolds and bring solutions to all the segments of the society and so do the lives of billions of people. Taking the right precautions and measures, we can restrict its impact and the scars it leaves. Henceforth, we must focus to build a better future so that the huge losses brought by the catastrophe can be revived quickly.

References

1. Alon, T., Doepke, M., Jane, O.R., &Tertilt, M. (2020)."The Impact of COVID-19 on Gender Equality."Covid Economics: Vetted and Real-Time Papers Issue, 4, 62– 85.
2. Centers for Disease Control and Prevention. (2021, May 21). "COVID-19 and Your Health".
3. Deborah, G. (2020). "Employment Trends and Future Prospects" (presentation at the 1st meeting of the G20 Employment Working Group, Saudi Arabia. Retrieved from https://www.ilo.org/wcmsp5/groups/public/—dgreports/—cabinet/documents/presentation/wcms_736015.pdf
4. Eurostat. (2018, June 20). Working from home in the EU.
5. ILO Monitor.(2020a). COVID-19 and the world of work.(1st Ed).
6. ILO Monitor.(2020b). COVID-19 and the world of work.(5th Ed).
7. ILO Monitor.(2021). COVID-19 and the world of work.(7th Ed). Updated estimates and analysis.
8. ILO. (2020c, March 26). Keys for effective teleworking during the COVID-19 pandemic.
9. ILO. (2020d, April, 30). Protecting migrant workers during the COVID-19 pandemic: Recommendations for policy-makers and constituents.
10. ILOSTAT database
11. International Labour Organization and Organisation for Economic Co-operation and Development, "Global Skills Trends, Training Needs and Lifelong Learning Strategies for the Future of Work". (June 2018). Retrieved from http://www.g20.utoronto.ca/2018/g20_global_skills_trends_and_lll_oecd-ilo.pdf
12. International Labour Organization, "Country Profiles", ILOSTAT database. Retrieved from https://ilostat.ilo.org/data/country-profiles/

13. Jeasakul, P. (2020). Considerations for Designing Temporary Liquidity Support to Businesses.Monetary and Capital Markets.

14. Monetary and Capital Markets."Central Bank Support to Financial Markets in the Coronavirus Pandemic".

15. Muller, T., &Schulten, T. (2020).Ensuring fair short-time work - a Europe an overview. ETUI (European Trade Union Institute), Policy Brief, N°7/ 2020, p. 1-12.

16. Norwegian Refugee Council. (2020, July). COVID-19 Impact Assessment Report Yemen.

17. OECD (2020, July 2). Paid sick leave to protect income, health and jobs through the COVID-19 crisis.OECD Policy Responses to Coronavirus (COVID-10).

18. OECD. (2019). Employment Outlook 2019: The Future of Work, OECD Publishing, Paris. Retrieved from https://doi.org/10.1787/9ee00155-en

19. Open Knowledge Repository. Monitoring COVID-19 Impacts on Households in Ethiopia: Results from a High Frequency Phone Survey of Households.

20. Page, J., Hinshaw, D., & McKay, B. (2021, February 26). "In Hunt for Covid-19 Origin, Patient Zero Points to Second Wuhan Market – The man with the first confirmed infection of the new coronavirus told the WHO team that his parents had shopped there". Retrieved from The Wall Street Journal.

21. Qian, M., & Jiang, J. (2020)."COVID-19 and social distancing.*Journal of Public Health*, 1–3. doi:10.1007/s10389-020-01321-z

22. Saint, M. A., Inanc, H., &Prinz, C. (2018). "Job Quality, Health and Productivity: An evidence-based framework for analysis". OECD Social, Employment and Migration Working Papers, No. 221, OECD Publishing, Paris. Retrieved from https://dx.doi.org/10.1787/a8c84d91-en

23. UNDP. (2020a, June 8). Impact socio-économique de la pandémie de la covid-19 au Sénégal.

24. UNDP.(2020b, April).Socio-Economic Impact of COVID-19 in Uganda. (April 2020).

25. United Kingdom, Government of 'Coronavirus Support for Employees, Benefit Claimants and Businesses'. (2020, March 16). Retrieved from https://www.gov.uk/government/news/coronavirus-support-for-employees-benefit-claimants-andbusinesses.

26. Walter, D. (2020). Implications of Covid-19 for Labour and Employment in India. *The Indian Journal of Labour Economics*, 63,47–51. https://doi.org/

10.1007/s41027-020-00255-0

27. World Health Organization.(2021, April 30). "Coronavirus disease (COVID-19): How is it transmitted?"

28. World Vision. (2020, May 29). COVID-19: Rapid Impact Assessment Bangladesh.

29. Zimmer, C. (2021, February 26). "The Secret Life of a Coronavirus – An oily, 100- nanometer-wide bubble of genes has killed more than two million people and reshaped the world. Scientists don't quite know what to make of it".

XIV

Covid-19 Pandemic: Issues of Employed Youth of Assam

Poppy Gogoi[1] and Dr. Jinamoni Saikia[2]
[1]Research Scholar and [2]Professor
Dept. of Human Development and Family Studies
College of Community Science, Assam Agricultural University, Jorhat-13, Assam
Email Id: jina_saikia@yahoo.com

Abstract

Recently the world is overshadowed by the covid-19 pandemic and is undergoing through the tragic loss of human life. Covid-19 is an infectious disease caused by severe acute respiratory syndrome coronavirus 2(SARS-CoV-2) which has been causing mayhem all over the world. It is one of the greatest challenges of the 21st century the world is facing right now. It is a major threat and crisis of the human health hasalso led worldwide socio-economic disruption. According to the International Labor Organization (ILO) 2020 report, the global unemployment rate has risen to around 25 million, while 364 million or more employees in India are at a risk of being adversely affected during lockdown. There is extreme rise in unemployment as many industries were closed due to which many workers had to lose their job and accommodation and were left with no choice other than returning to their native places. Youths were more vulnerableto unemployment during the pandemic due to lack of skills and experience. One of the significant aspects among employed youths of Assam is that some of them have become self employed by staying connected to the roots and nurturing their prevailing expertise, but as all the economic activities were halted during the pandemic, some people who were employed in different parts of the country have lost their jobs and those who were self-employed were also hampered as they are unable to operate their work. Therefore, the government should make laws and policies to ensure secure working conditions and equal treatment of workers regardless of their status and indulgence.

Keywords: Pandemic, covid-19, unemployment, youth

Introduction

The emergence of new unprecedented covid-19 was first detected in Wuhan Province of China in 2019 where the first case was reported in December 2019. Health experts believed that the new strain of corona virus is originated from bats. The World Health Organization has declared covid-19 a pandemic on 11th March, 2020 as the infection spread across many countries and territories in the world and by that time 118,000 confirmed cases of the corona virus in 110 countries were reported. In the month of January 2020, China had been the first country with a widespread outbreak followed by South Korea, Iran and Italy in February.The cases of covid-19 were at peak in the month of September 2020 in India but once again the rising cases of covid-19 from the first week of March 2021, indicated the arrival of the second wave of covid-19 disease. The new variant was first identified in United Kingdom (UK) and South Africa. Since April 2021, India became the worst covid-19 surge in the world with shortage of hospital beds, no oxygen and medicines and reported more than 20.65 lakh cases in the first half of April itself. The second wave of covid-19 has shattered the human life across the world. As of 31 May 2021, the covid-19 had spread in 210 countries and territories. It has infected around 171 million people globally and around 3.6 million people had died. The most severely affected countries include USA occupying the first position with highest number of cases while Brazil and India hold second and third position.

Keeping in view of the first and second wave of the pandemic, the Central Government of India had imposed nationwide lockdown on 24th March 2020 as a precautionary measure for 21 days which led to a halt in the state of all economic activities of the country.Again in 2021 due to rise in covid-19 cases, many states of India have imposed complete lockdown to tackle with the spread of second wave of covid-19. The lockdown has compelled all the schools, colleges, universities and other educational institutions to be closed as well as the cancellation of classes, examinations and entrance exams of all the schools, colleges and universities. Now the traditional mode of teaching has been shifted to online learning. It has also disrupted the economy of the country by closing the shops, office, banks, transportation services, other recreational centres etc. sparing the emergency services like hospitals, pharmacies, essential good shops, media and press due to which the common people suffered a lot.The covid-19 pandemic in the world has not only affected the health of people but has severely affected the economy of the country. According to the Ministry of Statistics, India's growth in the fourth quarter of fiscal year 2020 have fallen to 3.1 percent and has faced largest fall in the GDPthat is 24 percent ever between the month of April to June in the fiscal year 2021. Due to the disruptions emerged in the global market, the stock market of India is also witnessing volatility. The pandemic has resulted stress on supply chains and trade with other countries, collapsed hospitality and tourism industry, reduced consumer activity, decrease in government income and ultimately leading to unemployment of youth.

Covid-19 and employment

According to the document published by International Labour organisation (ILO, 3rd ed.) around 81 percent employed people in India are working in the informal sector with only 6.5 percent in the formal sector and 0.8 percent in the household sector.Around 20 percent of the Indian workforces are engaged in informal sector and micro, small and medium enterprises (Puri, 2020). According to International Labour Organization (ILO) 2020, it was estimated that there were around 164 million migrant workers worldwide which comprises almost 4.7 percent of the total labour force of the world. Amongst which, India continued to be the largest of origin of international migration with 17.5 million staying abroad (World Migration Report, 2020).

But during nationwide lockdown period, more than 1.06 crore migrant workers returned to their native places in India between the month of May and August 2020, as per the data compiled by Ministry of Labour and Employment.According to the government estimates, around 3.41 lakh migrant workers have returned to Assam during lockdown. Due to restrictions of public transportations thousands of migrants, some with their families, were seen walking or bicycling hundreds of kilometres to their native places (Pandey, 2020; Rashid, *et al.*, 2020).The labourers in the informal sector were likely to be the worst affected in terms of loss of employment and income following the COVID-19 lockdown as revealed by International Labour Organization (ILO) 2020. Many workers of informal sector were underprivileged, low skilled labours and, are the most vulnerable due to lack of social support and protection, exploitative working surroundings and inability to access health and other essential facilities.

According to Centre for Monitoring Indian Economy (CMIE), the unemployment rate of Assam has increased from 0.7 to 11.1 percent since April 2016 to April 2020. The lockdown has doubled the unemployment rate by closing down all the economic activities.Due to the immediate shutdown of businesses, almost all the migrant workers of Assam returned to their respective places due to lack of accommodation, risk in working conditions, no work leading to no money and no access to support measures such as food and other necessities.The youths are facing great psychological stress, over burden and huge loss during the lockdown period. Majority of the migrant workers who lost their employment were the daily wage labourers working in different manufacturing and construction industries while some of them were working as security guards in malls. Even though many of them have returned to work after the government has eased the restrictions but many are not willing to go back to their workplace and have opted many skilled and unskilled works in order to earn their livelihood. They have engaged themselves in trivial sources, as delivery boy under different services, salesman, security guards, working as wage earners, domestic workers, cook, carpentry, masonry, construction work etc. Youths who have high capital and land have started their own small scale farming sector while others have started in partnership.

Some educated migrants who have returned from foreign countries have started their own NGOs and companies in partnerships which are promoting people contributing significantly in diversified fields. There are NGO's who are working on imparting online education to the poor children and also children in remote areas during lockdown. Many have been working on delivering essential commodities such as food or grocery items and many have been sanitizing the public area. There are also many educated youths who were working in renowned companies of different parts of the country and have returned to their own place are continuing to work from home.Keeping in view of the pandemic and in order to maintain social distancing, the government of India had ordered to work from home for the benefit of the companies, enterprises, institutions etc. so that the employees can give their best at work within their comfort. It was intended to maintain the output and efficiency during the pandemic but some people are unable to give their best which has led to decrease in their efficiency and also productivity of the company. Work from home has negatively affected many employees because of reasons like - some were accustomed to the day-to-day routine and structure as that of working in an office environment, some were fond of physical interactions with colleagues, some people easily get distracted and hampered by household chores or disturbances caused by family members. Even though working from home, many workers of private sector are facing layoffs and pay cuts.

The pandemic has not only affected the migrant workers of Assam but also disrupted the economic conditions of the youth of Assam who were engaged under different sectors in Assam.

As Assam is mainly agriculturally based state and among all the productive sectors, agriculture makes the highest contribution to its domestic sectors, accounting for more than a third of Assam's income and employs 69% of workforce. Many youngsters have been engaged in agriculture, sericulture, pisciculture, poultry, piggery, apiculture, tea plantation, handloom, handicrafts etc. by connecting with the grassroots and identifying the demand and essentiality of local people and have focused on exporting and promoting the ethnic and local products. But the covid-19 which is a catastrophe has shaken the farming sector in Assam.The farmers have been facing huge loss from their farm due to restricted movements in transportation and trades. They were unable to sell their produce in the market due to closure of vegetable markets. The farmers have been facing threat to their livelihood as they are under the burden of loan taken from the bank and private money lenders for their cultivation which they usually pay off by selling the harvest. In order to run their families and manage an income, the farmers were desperately selling the crops or vegetables from door to door at the cheapest rates possible. Many of the farmers have even sold off their land or properties and some have given their land on lease to pay the monthly instalments to money lenders because of which the mental health of the farmers and other family members are heavily affected.

Livestock and poultry farmers were hit by the rumours on social media that consumption of chicken leads to coronavirus due to which there was a decrease in the demand of chicken supply. Some farmers had culled the chicks while many have sold their chicken at very cheap prices. Moreover, the farmers also have faced scarcity of feed during lockdown due to closure of retail shops and mills except essential items. Milk cooperatives, farms and individual producers of milk were severely affected across Assam. According to the Union minister of Animal husbandry, Diary and Fisheries, there was a loss of Rs 1,500 crore to 2,000 crores daily from the poultry industry. The shutdown of all hotels, restaurants and transportation of milk to the wholesale markets etc. in the state had forced dairy farmers to throw thousands of litres of milk each day on roads and river during lockdown as they could not sell it. Many milk farmers have laid off their employees to cut the cost due to drastic fall in sales.

Since Tea is one of the most important export commodities of India; even during the lockdown, tea garden workers continued to work as it was the peak time of harvesting the leaves. But the condition was exceedingly worst for the casual workers as they were on the verge of losing their jobs. They suffered the most having no work, no source of money and were running out of the resources to meet the family needs. Even in some industries, the permanent workers were also not paid their daily wages on time and rations such as rice, wheat flour, tea leaves which are a part of their weekly wages were also withdrawn during the lockdown period.

In Assam, weaving is considered to be the second most widely practiced activitymostly by girls and women after agriculture. They had been weaving traditional dresses and material enriched with beautiful motifs to sell directly to the customers, private stores or vendors and also to some cooperative societies and NGOs. But as the current situation is very challenging, their production and sales have stopped leading to stoppage in income generation and moreover their pre-existing contracts were getting over which has compelled the weaver to incur heavy losses. In Assam, bamboo is abundantly found in almost all villages. Therefore, some have engaged themselves in making variety of bamboo products. These kind of self-employment needs large number of labour force which means providing employment to many skilled and unskilled people thereby decreasing the rate of unemployment. But during lockdown, these weavers and craftsman were the victims of crisis as they may not possess sufficient resources especially financial and managerial and are not prepared for such kind of disruptions for longer period than expected.

Many educated youths who have completed courses in tourism, MBA, hotel management, etc. are engaged in travel, tourism and hospitality sector as Assam is a hub of natural resources and rich in biodiversity. Some have opened resorts, parks while some are working as travel agent, tour operator, tourist guide etc. and also engaged themselves in accommodation business and also business such as sports centres, cafeteria, bars, restaurants, hotels, etc. thus by creating job opportunities for many unemployed skilled and unskilled people of local area. But due to closed down of all the tourist places and cancellation of all the bookings for longer period, the industry has come to a standstill due to which some contractual staff had been laid off at some travel firms thus losing job.Employees of these business services or industries who in their daily life deals directly with people may experience stress and pressure due to the service they have to provide such as direct communication with the customers, handling their personal belongings etc. The employees may face the problems of getting infected, unstable employment, unpaid leave, overwork due to another employee leave etc. The stress can have negative impacts and work attitude (Kim, *et al.*, 2015) and negatively affect overall work performance (Akgunduz, 2015).

Now a days, many professional coursesare gaining pace among the youths. Many youths opt for these courses irrespective of their education level to become self-reliant and to secure appropriate jobs. Many youths acquiring these professional skills have started their own small-scale business setup or enterprises but are facing great challenges such as decrease in demand, breakdown of supply chains, cancellation of orders, raw material shortage and reduction in sales and profits.Moreover, these enterprises depend on routine business transactions and on small number of regular customers. In order to maintain the pandemic protocols, they are losing the regular customers and even though they can provide door to door services but most people are apprehensive of availing these services in fear of infection.

Moreover, the services like retail shops, food services and arts/ entertainment have provided the opportunities or gateway for jobs to younger generation or students working part time. But due to the pandemic and as per the covid guidelines the closure of academic institutions has forced the younger generation to leave their jobs making them unemployed and dependent on their families. Youths are the most hit due to sudden loss of education, closing down of entry level jobs in the labour market as well as internship and apprenticeship.

The pandemic has created new challenges for the protection of health along with safety of employment sector for future generation. Hence, future studies can consider these issues for more in-depth knowledge about the consequences of the pandemic on employment of youth of Assam.

Conclusions

From the above context it can be seen that the world is already facing a huge calamity due to the high spread of covid-19. And yet again, India is facing the second wave of coronavirus which is going to make the economic, social, political and cultural condition of the country fall into a grave and terrible situation. The unprecedented Covid-19 pandemic has not only disrupted the economy of the country butalso has brought the mental health problems among the youth. People have been undergoing through stress and anxiety due to fear of getting infected with covid-19, social isolation, loss of loved one and jobs. Many youths have been trying to overcome this situation through substance abuse during the pandemic. Policies to make strategies to provide resources, training and capacity building of people in different levels may minimize these problems. Adherence to strict rules and regulation in this regard also may be encouraged in government levels. The government of Assam should also focus and prioritize on employing the youths and maximize youth productivity as a covid-19 recovery process to improve the economic and sustainable growth of the state and the country. The non-government organizations as well as elite people of society can also venture to take up certain innovative measures to strengthen this most effected section of the society.The Indian society needs to work as one in these times of distress and despair to collaboratively uplift each other and successfully fight this pandemic.

References

1. Akgunduz, Y. (2015). The influence of self-esteem and role stress on job performance in hotel businesses. *International Journal of Contemporary Hospitality Management.*, 27(6): 1082–1099

2. Bordoloi, M. (2021, March 24). Assam assemble election 2021: Eyeing agripreneurship to secure future, youths seek govt backing for budding sector. Retrieved fromhttps://www.firstpost.com › Politics News

3. CDC (Centers for Disease Control and Prevention) (2020). Coronavirus disease 2019 (COVID-19) situation summary

1. Deb, K. (2020, April 30). How COVID-19 lockdown is forcing Assam farmers to dump harvest. Retrieved on 05/05/2021 from https://www.eastmojo.com ›

5. Economic impact of the covid-19 pandemic in India. In Wikipedia. https://en.m.wiipedia.org › wiki

6. Guha, P.; Islam, B. and Hussain, MA. (2020). COVID-19 lockdown and penalty of joblessness on income and remittances: A study of inter-state migrant labourers from Assam, India. *Journal of Public Affairs.* Retrieved on 05/05/2021 from https://doi.org/10.1002/pa.247https://thewire.in › labour › gov

7. PTI. (2021, March 14). These are the 5 most affected countries with highest number of covid-19 cases. Hindustan Times. Retrieved on 02/06/2021 from https://www.hindustantimes.com›

8. International Labour Organisation (ILO). (2020). ILO warns of COVID-19 migrant 'crisis within a crisis'. Retrieved on 09/05/2021 from https://www.ilo.org/global/ about-theilo/newsroom/news/WCMS_748992/lang–en/index.htm

9. International Labour Organisation (ILO). (2020). ILO monitor: COVID-19 and the world of work. 3rd ed.

1. Karmakar, R. (2020, March 30). Coronavirus lockdown |Dairy, vegetable farmers count losses. The Hindu. Retrieved from https://www.thehindu.com › News › National

11. Kim, S. S.; Im, J. and Hwang, J. (2015). The effects of mentoring on role stress, job attitude, and turnover intention in the hotel industry. *International Journal of Hospitality Management*, 48: 68–82.

12. Mint Analytics. (2020, May 1). Unemployment in Assam hits 19-month high of 11.1% in Apr 2020: CMIE Survey. https://www.livemint.com/news/india/unemployment-in-assam- hits-19-month-high-of-11-1-in-apr-2020-cmie-survey/amp-11588316041563.html

13. Pandey, V. (2020). The Covid-19 migrants who never got home, Delhi, India: BBC News

14. Puri, L. (2020). View: India should use migrant labour crisis to transform economy, society. The Economic Times

15. Rashid, O.; Anand, J. and Mahale, A. (2020). India coronavirus lockdown migrant workers and their long march to uncertainty. *The Hindu*. Retrieved on 24/05/2021 from https://www.thehindu.com

16. PTI.(2020, September 23). Over 1 crore migrant labourers return to home states on foot during Mar-Jun: Govt. *The Hindu*. Retrieved on 24/05/2021 from https://www.thehindu.com>news

17. PTI. (2021, May 9). Covid-19 Second wave: Here's a list of states that have imposed full lockdown. *The Indian Express*. Retrieved on 24/05/2021 from https://indianexpress.com

18. PTI. (2020, April 19).Milk cooperatives, dairy farms in Assam face problem due to lockdown restrictions. *The New Indian Express*. Retrieved on 24/05/2021 from https://www.newindianexpress.com › nation › apr › mil.

19. World Migration Report. (2020). UN migration. Geneva, Switzerland: International Organization for Migration

XV
Impact of COVID-19 on Employment of Migrant Workers

Poonam verma[1,] Dr. Shalini Agarwal[2] and Dr. Khwairakpam Sharmila[3]
[1]Research Scholar, [2]Associate Professor and [3]Assistant Professor
Department of Human Development and Family Studies,
Babasaheb Bhimrao Ambedkar University, Lucknow, Uttar Pradesh,
India
Email Id:pv115318@gmail.com

Abstract

This chapter stated a wide variety of necessary issues concerning the issue of having an impact on epidemics like COVID-19 on the migrant people. These influences are most heavy for low-profit households that are much less well-positioned to deal with revenue losses from a recession, don't have any number of revenue and don't have any social insurance plan obtainable. Most of these people earn very little, pretty a subsistence wage and don't have any choice to defend their earnings if they lose their jobs. Migrant people signify a large percentage of such inclined people. voluminous migrant people are predicted to be left unemployed in India thanks to the internment and resultant fear of recession. Several of the migrant employees have come to their village, and a lot of them are honestly awaiting the internment to be raised. The threat is mainly greater for human beings who are running in unorganized sectors, or these whose contracts are at the verge of completion. The internment and the resultant recession are additionally possible to hit contract people throughout quite a few of the industries. On the different hand, lockdown and social distancing measures are desiccation of jobs and incomes, whereas it's possible to disrupt the opposite. There's a necessity to relook at the countrywide migration policies, which might also reduce the strain amongst the migrants to come to their native place.

Key words: Migration Migrant labour COVID-19 Employment

Introduction

Each individual's temperament to measure the proper quantity of existence and overcome a problem used to be related to the wish to migrate alongside the route of human files (United Nations, 2006). By reducing state, monetary activities and incomes alternate by way of remittances, migrant labourers contributed to the engine of growth in the worldwide areas of organising areas (Ahn, 2004) and to the extent and enchantment of holiday spots in countries. It's calculable that there are 164 million migrant personnel worldwide, comprising 4.7% of the total labour stress on the planet (ILO, 2020a). Across nations, the Republic of India persisted in being the most vital U. S. setting up international migration with seventeen.5 million staying in distant areas (World Migration Report, 2020). The indoor migration (inter and intrastate) in the Republic of India multiplied from 314.5 million to 455.8 million between 2001 and 2011, with the variety of migrant imperative personnel rising from a hundred to 139.1 million in 2011 (Census of the Republic of India, 2001, 2011). The Uttar Pradesh, Bihar, Jharkhand, Odisha, Madhya Pradesh, Rajasthan, Chhattisgarh, provinces and, therefore, the end, consequently, the proximity of the most quintessential sources of workingage Indian people. The World Health Organization migrated to one-of-a-kind Indian states in search of remunerative engagement (Singh, Patel, Chaudhary, & Mishra, 2020). Besides its world charge as a rustic origin, the indoor migration of labourers has performed a critical function in each and every section of the Indian economy, especially in the informal quarters and small, tiny and medium enterprises. Nearly two hundredths of the Indian work force are engaged in informal sectors.

Though migrant labourers make a contribution, notably to the financial sector as invisible voters, a range of them, mainly low-virtuoso labourers, get pleasure from wholly restrained human and labour rights and face exploitive working conditions (Diop, 2010). Many lookup research in the previous expressed the vulnerability of migrant labourers relative to native counterparts (Bustamante, 2011; Derose, Escarce, & Lurie, 2007; Mehra, 2017). Social insecurity and excessive deprivation of fundamental offerings are common amongst migrant labourers (Bhagat, Reshmi, Sahoo, Roy, & Govil, 2020; Mukherjee, Paul, & Pathan, 2009). The close by gadgets used to be normally denied adequate fitness care, nutrition, housing, and sanitation (Nair & Verma, 2020).

COVID-19 has been notably brutal to the migrant workers. quite eighty per cent of them lost their employment and alternative means that of livelihoods. because the Indian State set to prevent trains and bus operations hurriedly, several necessitous and desperate migrant workers started walking to their home cities and villages. Later, once pictures of walking migrant workers on highways, cases of accidents and deaths, from time to time thanks to starvation started flashing, eventually their issues became headlines of the national and international media. the govt. of Republic of India, by currently unsettled with these developments, modified its position and intra-State movement of workers was permitted; afterwards restricted variety of train and bus services were additionally began to carry stranded inter-state workers to their homes. withal, by then, tens of thousands of workers have/had most well-liked walking thanks to either inconvenience or terribly restricted variety of trains. Reports have delivered to our notice instances of migrants being asked to pay full transportation that several of them, of course, couldn't afford.

Migrant workers

The **migrant**manpower consists of home employees (who both work part-time or live-in both socio-economic type or elite home), cart pullers, protection guards, taxi drivers, shipping boys, relaxation room cleaners, and enterprise employees (brick-kilns, stone quarries, and mines), small-scale change (leather add-ons, diamond cutting, garment factories, textiles, jewellery-making, etc.), and agricultural people (sugarcane cutting, chili manufacturing, they left their native houses, particularly for financial reasons. A number of these migrants are, moreover, rapt for social reasons marriage, and transferring to households and choosing social motives (business, education).

The share of migrant manpower amongst the total manpower inside the important sectors. Like primary sectors, producing, public services, construction, historic services, cutting-edge services.

What is covid-19?

According to World Health Organization (WHO) web site, "on thirty one December 2019, World Health Organization was advised and learnt of cases of respiratory illness of unknown cause in urban center town, China". A completely unique corona virus was recognized and acknowledged because the basis by Chinese authorities on seven Jan 2020 and was quickly named "2019-nCoV."Corona viruses (CoV) area unit a significant cluster of viruses that cause infection unsteady from the respiratory disorder to additional severe diseases and extreme maladies. a completely unique corona virus (nCoV) could be a new tension and pressure that has not been erstwhile acknowledged within the past to the people (WHO).

The appearance and development of the present worldwide pandemic, Covid-19, has to this point been a danger likewise as risk to the worldwide network of voters. COVID-19 or novel corona virus could be a variant of the corona group of viruses that causes infection known as respiratory illness on the people they contaminate (Buheji etal, 2020).

The virus is primarily transmitted through coughing or physiological reaction on people (Buheji et. al, 2020). Sengupta and Jha (2020) states that the pandemic caused by the corona virus un wellness (COVID 19), the severest well-being crisis of our times, is prepared to disturb social, economic and political systems and lives round the world. During this chapter, the impact of corona virus on social and financial set-up on rural migrants in Asian country can be lined. With the absence of any cheap immunization, most governments have mandatory dead forced lockdowns to regulate the event of the virus inflicting infection (Buheji et.al, 2020).

India responded to COVID- 19

Prime Minister Narendra Modi obligatory a 21-day obligatory imprisonment from March twenty-four, 2020 and intended Indians to practise likewise the following: social separation and hand hygiene through laundry hands of times (Nilsen, 2020). He requested the people to stay at anywhere where they're (Nilsen, 2020). Sengupta and Jha (2020). States that as preventive moderation measures, India started strict controls since March 2020, requesting 1.3 billion people to stay reception for the fundamental quantity of imprisonment except if engaged in essential and basic services. Through a mixture of management actions that enclosed constraint on movement and movement of producing factories and work environments, nations area unit making an attempt and dealing to "flatten the curve" that's decreasing the COVID -19 cases and to stop the preventive and collapse of the aid system of India (Sengupta and Jha, 2020). An issue still remains within the mind of the authors that "Who is additional susceptible to this virus?" The migrant labourers or staff area unit is thought to be the first susceptible to this virus. Hence, the chapter can specialize in rural migrants and their impacts.

Employment and COVID- 19

Studies exhibit those employment provisions on hand in the very nearby, even at low income scale, returned seasonal misery migration. As an example, examining preliminary inspection know-how from 3 states of Bharat (Imbert and Papp (2018)), we show that the furnish of employment in native building migration regardless of the top income available in the villages. The use of provisions avail-able locally for migrants has to be compelled to be robust so as to scale back again the hole between the monetary obtain at providing and at the destination. The native monetary attain era moreover comes with extra assurances and proximity to security simply in case of unheard-of situations like COVID-19. This will be performed both by means of growing "NREGA" or by means of growing extra by means of augmented authorities disbursal into native public work.

Migration and Employment condition in India

Generally, stoop inside the vacation spot reduces the wide variety of migrants, reduces remittances, and disrupts migrant structures (Curran et al., 2016). Disrupting migrant systems The Economic Survey 2016–2017 had calculated that over 9 million of us migrate yearly among the country, and most of such migration is for a job or education. Whereas Delhi, accompanied by using the city center, is the excessive vacation spot for migrants, many of us rectangular measures migrate to the cities in the southern states, like the metropolis, Chennai, etc. The largest variety of these migrants is from the provinces of the province, UP, the geographical vicinity and Assam.

International migration constitutes round two. It constitutes 6.6 per cent of the full migration (Census, 2011). As per International Labour Organization (2018), there are in fact over thirty million Indians overseas, with over 9 million Indian migrants focused inside the GCC place (now known as the Cooperation Council for the Arab States of the Gulf). Over ninety per cent of Indian migrant staff, most of whom are low- and semi-skilled staff, are from the Gulf vicinity and South-East Asia. The contribution of migrant staff, every extraordinarily masterful and low masterful one, has a semiconductor diode to the Republic of India turning into the best recipient of remittances in the world, with over US$62.7 billion acquired in 2016 (ILO, 2018).

Unemployment and poverty

About 450 million casual body of workers comprising ninety-nine percentage of India's manpower weren't allowed to take personal paid leaves (Sengupta, Jha, 2020). A better phase of them vicinity unit migrant personnel UN corporation location unit at the sting of the emergency or disaster during the internment as soon as work from the domestic will become the new standard all through the world thanks to the epidemic. Varied amongst these inter-state migrants picked to run many kilometers in the hope of returning to their native locations (Slater et.al 2020)," Among them, the worry of staying hungry over ordinary wage loss overshadowed their anxiousness and misery of the virus (Ganguly, 2020).

Conclusions

This chapter presents perception into the employment of migrant people due to the COVID-19 pandemic. There was once failure of the Indian facet the place a prior method dealing with migrants, people in the casual sector, and livelihood selections for each day wage earners, migrant employees was once absolutely lacking. There was an absence of appropriate preparation before the first declaration of the nationwide lockdown on 24 March, 2020, thereby resulting in discrimination among migrants, overall health and well-being of migrants deteriorated in the absence of any measures taken by the Government. These migrants were facing social pressure of poverty, loss of employment, livelihood, and stigmatization and were alienated by the countrymen left alone on roads to meet their fate where many of the migrants lost their lives. Although the Government initiatives were taken which came very late, and many migrants had to lose their lives while going back home. The truth is that rural migrants are a very important and vital part of our economy without which both rural and urban areas will not be able to sustain.

References

1. United Nations (2006). International migration and development. Report of the Secretary-General for the 60th Session of the UN General Assembly, May, A/60/871 (New York).
2. Ahn P. S. (Ed.). (2004). Migrant workers and human rights out-migration from South Asia. New Delhi, India: International Labour Organization, Sub regional Office for South Asia
3. International Labour Organization (ILO) . (2020a). ILO warns of COVID-19 migrant 'crisis within a crisis' Retrieved from https://www.ilo.org/global/about-the-
4. World Migration Report.(2020). *UN migration.* Geneva, Switzerland: International Organization for Migration.
5. Singh, S. K. , Patel, V. , Chaudhary, A. , & Mishra, N. (2020). Reverse migration of Labourers amidst COVID-19. *Economic and Poilitical Weekly,* 55(19), 28–31
6. Puri, L. (2020, June 4). View: India should use migrant labour crisis to transform economy, society.
7. Diop, A. (2010). International labour migration: A rights-based approach. Geneva, Switzerland: International Labour Organization.
8. Bustamante, J. A. (2011). Extreme vulnerability of migrants: The cases of the United States and Mexico. *Migraciones Internacionales,*
9. Bhagat, R. B. , Reshmi, R. S. , Sahoo, H. , Roy, A. K. , & Govil, D. (2020). The COVID-19, migration and livelihood in India. A Background Paper for Policy Makers,

10. Nair, S. & Verma, D (2020, May 19). A policy framework for India's Covid-19 migration. Bloomberg Quint.

11. Rituparna Bhattacharyya, Pranjit Kumar Sarma, 30 September 2020, COVID-19 and India's labour migrants crisis, *International Journal of creativity and change.*

12. S. Udhaya Kumar,D. Thirumal Kumar et. al, 20 may 2020, The Rise and Impact of COVID-19 in India,

13. M. Buheji et.al, (2020), The Extent of COVID-19 Pandemic Socio-Economic Impact on Global Poverty. A Global Integrative Multidisciplinary Review. American Journal of Economics.

14. Sengupta & Jha (2020). Social Policy and impoverished migrants Challenges and prospects in Locked Down India. The International Journal of Community and Social Development.

15. Sengupta, & Jha (2020). Social Policy and impoverished migrants Challenges and prospects in Locked Down India. The International Journal of Community and Social Development.

16. , Alf, Gunvald,2020, Covid 19 and India's Development Crisis. African HSS

17. Imbert, Clement and Papp, John. 2018. "Costs and Benefits of Seasonal Migration: Evidence from India." The Warwick Economics Research Paper Series (TWERPS) 1161, University of Warwick.

18. Curran, S. R., Irons, J., Garip, F. (2016). Economic shock and migration: Differential economics effects, migrant responses, and migrant cumulative causation in Thailand. Sociol Dev (Oakl),

19. ILO. (2018). Indian Labour Migration. International Labour Organization.

20. Slater J, Masih N (2020) March 28 In India, the world's biggest lockdown has forced migrants to walk hundreds of miles home

21. Ganguly, M., Goli, S., Ganguly, D., & Misra, S. (2020). Munich Personal RePEc Archive India's COVID-19.

XVI

Management of COVID Oriented Hypoxia with Oxygenated Drinking Water

Dr. Lok Mani Gupta
Senior Homoeopathic Physician
Gupta Homoeo Clinic, Agrasen Bazar, Kota, Rajasthan, India

Abstract

During the second wave of COVID-19, mostly patients were suffering from hypoxia. At that time oxygen demand was very high and it was difficult to fulfil the increased oxygen need due to unavailability of apt medical support and oxygen. Therefore, this study was initiated with the idea that oxygenation of drinking water might be helpful to mitigate this oxygen demand of people and help them to improve their oxygen saturation level. Study was conducted in Kota City, Rajasthan in three distinct phases namely (i) identification/ assessment of level of dissolved oxygen in drinking water; (ii) oxygenation of drinking water and (iii) Assessment of effect of oxygenated water on patients. Results of this study indicated that dissolved oxygen level of oxygenated water was way higher than the normal drinking water supplied by municipality and the regular consumption of this oxygenated water was helpful to improve the oxygen saturation of a person. This study will be proved as a milestone in this area. If the model created in this study will be used at large level, it will not only fulfil the oxygen demand created in COVID hypoxic patients as well as it will create many employment opportunities at commercial level.

Key words: Oxygenated water, Drinking water, Oxygenation process, Dissolved oxygen, COVID management, COVID oriented hypoxia

Introduction

Atmospheric reduction of Oxygen due to continuous depletion of Greenery is the hot topic and being discussed most that the optimum saturation of Oxygen is regularly decreasing. The level of Oxygen in Air varies from place to place like hills, forests, rural areas and urban areas. As the OXYGEN level of air is regularly decreasing, it is supposed to be 21 instead of 22 in general and in diminishing trend from lush greenery to villages where it is around 16 and metro cities where found to be decreased up to a level of 13 only because of gradual Deforestation, Decreasing Agriculture lands, Industrial, house hold environmental pollution and Use of various harmful chemicals. Similarly the Water sources like Rivers and Underground Water is getting pollutants by virtue of City Drainage system and infiltration of Chemicals deep in earth and flowing water streams.

During the second wave of COVID-19 pandemic (third, fourth week of April 21 and first week of May 21) was most drastic, tragic and at its peak level. Most of the victims being middle aged youngsters irrespective of their cast, creed and sex. As it was very difficult to get them hospitalised and provide with apt medical support and Oxygen. Shortage of oxygen was at its peak and people were dying due to reduced oxygen saturation in body. Suddenly an idea flashed in researcher's mind and he immediately started working on it. The idea was 'how to improve oxygen concentration in water. All people drink at least 3-4 litre water daily to sustain their life in a healthy way. If level of oxygen can be improved in this water, it means some oxygen demand of a person can be fulfilled via this oxygenated drinking water.

Here comes the concept of dissolved oxygen. The oxygen dissolved in water due to diffusion from air, aeration of water and as a by-product of photosynthesis of plants is known as the dissolved oxygen. All the aquatic animals along with fishes used this dissolved oxygen for breathing because they cannot separate oxygen from water. They use gills for respiratory function that helps them to inhale oxygen dissolved in water. Biologically speaking, however, the level of oxygen is a much more important measure of water quality than faecal coliform. Dissolved oxygen is essential for the survival of all organisms (invertebrates and vertebrates). Moreover, oxygen affects a vast number of other water indicators, not only biochemical but aesthetic ones like the odour, clarity and taste. Consequently, oxygen is perhaps the most well established indicator of water quality (Dunn et al, 2016). Therefore, this study was initiated with the following objectives:

1. To analyse the level of dissolved oxygen parts per million (DO ppm) in drinking water
2. To improve/ enhance oxygen concentration of drinking water
3. To enhance the oxygen saturation of patients using oxygenated water

Material and Methods

Cross sectional research design was used in present study. This study was conducted in Kota City, Rajasthan. Study was divided into three phases.

Phase I- Identification/ assessment of level of dissolved oxygen in drinking water:

Four different samples of drinking water, i.e., (i) regular drinking water supplied by municipality, (ii) alum water, (iii) boiled water and (iv) cold water were taken and their level of dissolved oxygen was assessed using chemical analytic kit to measure dissolved oxygen ppm of drinking water. This chemical analytic kit consists as follows-

1. Two different labelled Chemicals namely reagent 1& reagent 2
2. One shade card
3. One test tube (for the sake of comparison and contingency we purchased few more test tubes.)
4. One empty syringe
5. One small bottlebrush.
6. Literature brochure giving guidelines to proceed on for the requisite tests.

Special instruction:

This product is a colour comparison technology based and intended to test the dissolved oxygen levels of clear colourless waters.

Most excitedly but keeping all due precautions we started the process with utmost care.

Precautions

1. Wash the test vials properly before and after use.
2. Test the samples as soon as possible after collecting it from the source.

Test procedure

1. Fill the test vial up till the neck with the water supplied directly from the source.
2. Add 5 drops of DO reagent 1 followed by 5 drops of DO reagent 2, holding the dropper of the bottle as close as possible with the sample. "Do not let the dropper tip touch the sample"
3. Close the cap and mix it gently for 5 seconds.
4. Leave the vial for 5 minutes, mix the contents again gently for 5 seconds and compare the colour with the shade card.

Phase II- Oxygenation of drinking water:

For oxygenation of water, the model of fish aquarium was applied in this experiment, where an air pump was used to pump the air in water and creates turbulence, which was supposed to be in working condition 24*7 for fish to survive.

Model creation:

A steel tank of approximately 10 litres was taken which was filled three fourth with the regular drinking water that is being supplied by municipality in Kota City, Rajasthan. Researcher attached the air pump working with it, covered it with a sieve and left it over night. After that level of dissolved oxygen of oxygenated water was assessed using the same procedure used in phase I.

Phase III- Assessment of effect of oxygenated water on patients:

After oxygenation process of regular drinking water supplied by municipality, this oxygenated water was given to post COVID or COVID asymptomatic patients to assess the change in their level of oxygen saturation. Four different groups of patients were made. Each group had 5 patients. They drink only this oxygenated water for next 5 days and then their level of oxygen saturation was checked.

Hypothesis

1. Level of dissolved oxygen is same in different samples of drinking water.
2. Level of dissolved oxygen in regular drinking water is lower than the oxygenated water.
3. Level of oxygen saturation of patients improves by regular drinking of oxygenated water.

Results and Discussions

Results indicate that level of dissolved oxygen in regular tap water supplied by municipality was 1 ppm. Usually it is said that alum water is better than normal drinking water as it purifies the water as well as have certain beneficial properties within it. This hypothesis was also assessed in present study and the results proved that alum not only purify the water as it separate impurities from water but also it improves the level of dissolved oxygen of water in some amount. Experiment results show that dissolved oxygen level of alum water was 2 ppm which was higher than the dissolved oxygen level of normal tap water.

Previous researches concluded that oxygen level of water reduced if it is too hot. Temperature plays an important role in survival of aquatic life. Fish are cold blooded animals, hence, their metabolic rate increases in higher temperature and they need more oxygen to survive. Evidence indicates that for diverse fish population at least 4-5 ppm of dissolved oxygen is required (Oram, 2014). Present study results are in line with the results of previous scientific researches. An inverse relation of dissolved oxygen ppm was found with the temperature. The values of dissolved oxygen level in cold water and hot water were 1 ppm and 2 ppm respectively illustrating that cold water contains higher values of dissolved oxygen level.

The value of dissolved oxygen of oxygenated water prepared using special apparatus is higher than all the samples of drinking water. The dissolved oxygen level of oxygenated water was 4 ppm indicating that this apparatus can play important role in oxygenation of water. The result supports the hypothesis that normal drinking water contains lower level of dissolved oxygen than the oxygenated water.

Being a senior homoeopathic physician, researcher knows a homoeopathic medicine- carboveg 30, commonly known as oxygen cylinder of homoeopathy and is used successfully in the condition of cyanosis. This medicine was prescribed during COVID-19 to bring up and maintain the oxygen saturation in Hypoxic patients. Researcher thought that addition of this medicine carboveg – 30, might also improves dissolved oxygen level of water; to verify the same hypothesis, he did the experiment with oxygenated water, with and without carboveg 30. The result of this experiment showed that the dissolved oxygen level of oxygenated water without carboveg 30 was around 4 ppm while that with carboveg 30 was 5 ppm. These results also proves the theory that carboveg 30 is the oxygen cylender in Homoeopathic medicines.

In last phase of this study, the prepared oxygenated water was supplied to COVID asymptomatic/ post COVID patients whom oxygen saturation level SPO_2 was in between 90-92. All the patients drank only this oxygenated water for 5 days. The oxygenated water was given to them as per their groups in different time slots. Results of this experiment were amazing as within 5 days after consumption, the oxygen saturation values of these patients were raised to 94-96. It is evident from the results of present study that regular consumption of oxygenated water can be used as a very good medium to control the hypoxia in COVID patients. These results are supported by many studies saying that oxygen can be absorbed through gastrointestinal tract via the permeation through the vessels therein to improve the need of oxygen in human body as the fishes do using the blood vessels in their gills (Kimberly et al, 2020; Fleming et al, 2017; Naughton et al, 2007).

Conclusions

Dissolved oxygen plays an important role in maintaining quality of water. If a person wants to be healthy, he needs to drink plenty of good quality water daily. Results of this study illustrates that oxygenation of drinking water improved the level of dissolved oxygen in water samples and the consumption of this oxygenated water enhanced the oxygen saturation SPO_2 of COVID asymptomatic/ post COVID patients in very few days. When body need of the oxygen cannot be fulfilled by lungs due to various reasons, the method proposed in present study can be used and is very helpful to increase the survival rate of an individual. This invention is not only very useful in medical area but it is also useful in daily life to maintain normal oxygen saturation of a person as well as it will create many employment opportunities to make the community self dependent and self empower consequently make them sustainable in terms of health as well as wealth.

Acknowledgement

My daughter Dr. Khushboo Gupta who is PhD Food and Nutrition supported my idea to measure this DO ppm scientifically. I took assistance of my son Er Saurabh Gupta and daughter Er Surbhee Gupta M Tech Nenotechnology to manage the required equipments, chemicals and observations. At last I am thankful to Almighty Goddess, whom blessings made my endeavour successful.

References

1. Oram, B. (2014). *Stream Water Quality – Importance of Temperature.* Retrieved from https://www.water-research.net/index.php/stream-water-quality-importance-of-temperature

2. McNaughton LR, Kenney S, Siegler J, Midgley AW, Lovell RJ, Bentley DJ. The effect of superoxygenated water on blood gases, lactate, and aerobic cycling performance. *Int J Sports Physiol Perform* 2007; **2**(4): 377- 385.

3. Fleming N, Vaughan J, Feeback M. Ingestion of oxygenated water enhances lactate clearance kinetics in trained runners. *J IntSoc Sports Nutr* 2017; **14**: 9.

4. Dunn J-O, Mythen M, Grocott M. Physiology of oxygen transport. *BJA Educ* 2016; **16**(10): 341- 348.

5. Kimberly L. Desmond, Sofia E. Chavez, Editorial for "Effect of Drinking Oxygenated Water Assessed by in vivo MRI Relaxometry", Journal of Magnetic Resonance Imaging, 10.1002/jmri.27239, **52**, 3, (729-730), (2020).

www.ingramcontent.com/pod-product-compliance
Lightning Source LLC
Chambersburg PA
CBHW031456160726
47994CB00005B/2052